bbq
food

bbq food

MURDOCH BOOKS

Contents

Skewers

Pork skewers in green ginger wine and soy marinade with chargrilled spring onion bulbs

800 g (1 lb 12 oz) pork fillets, trimmed
1 tablespoon finely grated fresh ginger
2 garlic cloves, finely chopped
1 tablespoon finely chopped preserved ginger in syrup
60 ml (¼ cup) green ginger wine (see Note)
2½ tablespoons kecap manis
½ teaspoon sesame oil
1 tablespoon oil
8 bulb spring onions, green parts removed, quartered
1 tablespoon olive oil
coriander (cilantro) sprigs

Cut the pork into 12 cm x 2.5 cm (5 inch x 1 inch) strips and put them in a non-metallic bowl with the ginger, garlic, preserved ginger, green ginger wine, kecap manis and oils, turning the meat to make sure it is evenly coated. Cover and refrigerate the bowl, and leave it to marinate for at least 2 hours, or overnight. Soak 12 wooden skewers in cold water for 1 hour, then thread four pork strips into an S-shape onto each skewer. Cover the skewers and refrigerate until you are ready to start cooking.

Preheat the barbecue to medium direct heat. Toss the spring onions with the olive oil and season them with salt and freshly ground black pepper. Cook them on the flat plate for 10 minutes, or until they are softened and well browned. When the spring onions are nearly cooked, put the kebabs on the chargrill plate and grill them for 2 minutes on each side, or until the pork is just cooked through and glazed. Garnish the skewers with coriander sprigs and serve them immediately with the spring onion.

Serves 4

Note: Green ginger wine is a sweet, fortified wine with a distinctive ginger flavour which originated in Britain.

Beef kebabs with mint yoghurt dressing

1 kg (2 lb 4 oz) lean beef fillet, cubed
125 ml (½ cup) olive oil
80 ml (⅓ cup) lemon juice
1 tablespoon chopped rosemary
2 small red onions, cut into wedges
200 g (7 oz) slender eggplants (aubergines), sliced

Mint yoghurt dressing
250 g (1 cup) plain yoghurt
1 garlic clove, crushed
1 small Lebanese (short) cucumber, grated
2 tablespoons chopped mint

Put the beef in a non-metallic bowl. Combine the olive oil, lemon juice and rosemary and pour over the beef. Cover and refrigerate for 2 hours.

To make the mint yoghurt dressing, mix together the yoghurt, garlic, cucumber and mint and season with salt and pepper.

Drain the beef and thread onto long metallic skewers, alternating pieces of beef with the onion wedges and slices of eggplant.

Cook the kebabs on a hot, lightly oiled barbecue grill or flat plate, turning often, for 5–10 minutes, or until the beef is cooked through and tender. Serve with the dressing.

Makes 8 kebabs

Tofu kebabs with miso pesto

1 large red capsicum (pepper),
    cubed
12 button mushrooms, halved
6 pickling onions, quartered
3 zucchini (courgettes), cut into
    chunks
450 g (1 lb) firm tofu, cubed
125 ml (½ cup) light olive oil
3 tablespoons light soy sauce
2 garlic cloves, crushed
2 teaspoons grated fresh ginger

Miso pesto
90 g (½ cup) unsalted roasted
    peanuts
60 g (2 cups) coriander (cilantro)
    leaves
2 tablespoons white miso paste
2 garlic cloves
100 ml (3½ fl oz) olive oil

If using wooden skewers, soak them in water for 30 minutes to prevent scorching. Thread the vegetables and tofu alternately onto 12 skewers, then place in a large non-metallic dish.

Mix together the olive oil, soy sauce, garlic and ginger, then pour half over the kebabs. Cover and leave to marinate for 1 hour.

To make the miso pesto, finely chop the peanuts, coriander leaves, miso paste and garlic in a food processor. Slowly add the olive oil while the machine is still running and blend to a smooth paste.

Cook the kebabs on a hot, lightly oiled barbecue flat plate or grill, turning and brushing with the remaining marinade, for 4–6 minutes, or until the edges are slightly brown. Serve with the miso pesto.

Serves 4

Garlic and mint lamb skewers with almond couscous and yoghurt sauce

8 lamb fillets, trimmed and cut
    into 2.5 cm (1 inch) cubes
2 tablespoons olive oil
80 ml (⅓ cup) lemon juice
2 garlic cloves, crushed
2 teaspoons dried mint leaves

Yoghurt sauce
250 g (1 cup) thick Greek-style
    yoghurt
1 garlic clove, crushed

Almond couscous
370 g (2 cups) instant couscous
1 tablespoon olive oil
500 ml (2 cups) chicken stock
40 g (1½ oz) butter
2 teaspoons ras el hanout (if you
    are unable to find it, see page 83
    for a recipe to make your own)
35 g (¼ cup) currants, soaked in
    warm water for 10 minutes
60 g (½ cup) slivered almonds,
    toasted
25 g (½ cup) chopped mint leaves

Put the lamb in a non-metallic bowl with the olive oil, lemon juice, garlic and mint. Stir the pieces around until well coated and season with black pepper. Cover and refrigerate for at least 4 hours, or overnight.

Make the yoghurt sauce by mixing the yoghurt and garlic in a small bowl, then refrigerate it until you are ready to use it.

Put the couscous in a heatproof bowl, drizzle it with the olive oil and season well with salt. Bring the chicken stock to the boil and pour it over the couscous, then cover the bowl and leave it for 10 minutes to absorb the stock. Add the butter and fluff it through with a fork until it has melted and the grains are separated. Stir in the ras el hanout, currants, almonds and mint, and season to taste with salt and pepper.

Soak eight wooden skewers in cold water for 1 hour, then thread the lamb onto them and season well. Preheat the barbecue to medium–high direct heat and grill the skewers for about 3–4 minutes on each side, or until they are cooked to your liking. Serve the skewers on a bed of couscous with the yoghurt sauce.

Serves 4

Involtini of swordfish

1 kg (2 lb 4 oz) swordfish,
  skin removed, cut into four
  5 cm (2 inch) pieces
3 lemons
80 ml (⅓ cup) olive oil
1 small onion, chopped
3 garlic cloves, chopped
2 tablespoons chopped capers
2 tablespoons chopped pitted
  Kalamata olives
35 g (⅓ cup) finely grated Parmesan
  cheese
120 g (1½ cups) fresh breadcrumbs
2 tablespoons chopped parsley
1 egg, lightly beaten
24 fresh bay leaves
2 small white onions, quartered and
  separated into pieces
2 tablespoons lemon juice, extra

Cut each swordfish piece horizontally into four slices to give you 16 slices in total. Place each piece between two pieces of plastic wrap and roll gently with a rolling pin to flatten without tearing. Cut each piece in half to give 32 pieces.

Peel the lemons with a vegetable peeler. Cut the peel into 24 even pieces. Squeeze the lemons to give 3 tablespoons of juice.

Heat 2 tablespoons olive oil in a pan, add the onion and garlic, and cook over medium heat for 2 minutes. Place in a bowl with the capers, olives, Parmesan, breadcrumbs and parsley. Season, add the egg and mix to bind.

Divide the stuffing among the fish pieces and, with oiled hands, roll up to form parcels. Thread four rolls onto each of eight skewers alternating with the bay leaves, lemon peel and onion.

Mix the remaining oil with the lemon juice in a bowl. Cook the skewers on a hot flat plate for 3–4 minutes each side, basting with the oil and lemon mixture. Serve with a little extra lemon juice drizzled over the top.

Serves 4

Sweet-and-sour
pork kebabs

1 kg (2 lb 4 oz) pork fillets, cubed
1 large red capsicum (pepper),
   cubed
1 large green capsicum (pepper),
   cubed
425 g (15 oz) tin pineapple pieces,
   drained, juice reserved
250 ml (1 cup) orange juice
3 tablespoons white vinegar
2 tablespoons soft brown sugar
2 teaspoons chilli garlic sauce
2 teaspoons cornflour (cornstarch)

Soak wooden skewers in water for
30 minutes to prevent scorching.
Thread pieces of meat alternately with
pieces of capsicum and pineapple
onto the skewers. Mix the pineapple
juice with the orange juice, vinegar,
sugar and sauce. Place the kebabs in
a shallow non-metallic dish and pour
half the marinade over them. Cover
and refrigerate for at least 3 hours,
turning occasionally.

Put the remaining marinade in a small
saucepan. Mix the cornflour with
1 tablespoon of the marinade until
smooth, then add to the pan. Stir over
medium heat until the mixture boils
and thickens. Transfer to a bowl,
cover the surface with plastic wrap
and leave to cool.

Cook the kebabs on a hot, lightly
oiled flat plate or grill for 15 minutes,
turning occasionally, until tender.
Serve with the sauce.

Serves 6

Satay chicken

500 g (1 lb 2 oz) chicken thigh fillets,
   cut into 1 cm (½ inch) wide strips
1 garlic clove, crushed
2 teaspoons finely grated fresh ginger
3 teaspoons fish sauce

Satay sauce
2 teaspoons peanut oil
4 red Asian shallots, finely chopped
4 garlic cloves, crushed
2 teaspoons finely chopped fresh
   ginger
2 small red chillies, seeded and finely
   chopped
125 g (½ cup) crunchy peanut buttor
185 ml (¾ cup) coconut milk
2 teaspoons soy sauce
2 teaspoons grated palm sugar or
   soft brown sugar
1½ tablespoons fish sauce
1 fresh kaffir (makrut) lime leaf
1½ tablespoons lime juice

Put the chicken, garlic, ginger and fish sauce in a bowl and turn the chicken so that it is well coated. Cover the bowl and leave it in the refrigerator for 1 hour. Soak 12 wooden skewers in cold water for 1 hour.

To make the satay sauce, heat the oil in a saucepan over medium heat, then add the shallot, garlic, ginger and chilli. Stir the mixture constantly with a wooden spoon for 5 minutes, or until the shallots are golden. Reduce the heat to low, add the remaining sauce ingredients and simmer for 10 minutes, or until the sauce has thickened. Remove the lime leaf and keep the sauce warm while you cook the chicken.

Preheat the barbecue chargrill plate to medium–high direct heat. Thread two or three chicken strips onto each skewer, without crowding them, and grill the chicken for 10 minutes, or until it is cooked through, turning after 5 minutes. Serve the skewers with the satay sauce. Delicious with cucumber salad (see page 350).

Serves 4

Scallop and fish rosemary skewers with marjoram dressing and chargrilled radicchio salad

2 tablespoons marjoram leaves
1 tablespoon lemon juice
80 ml (1/3 cup) olive oil, plus extra,
   for brushing
7 g (1/4 cup) chopped flat-leaf
   (Italian) parsley
8 long firm rosemary branches
600 g (1 lb 5 oz) firm white fish fillets,
   cut into 3 cm (1 1/4 inch) cubes
16 scallops with roe attached
2 heads radicchio, green outer leaves
   removed, cut into 8 wedges
50 g (1 3/4 oz) rocket (arugula) leaves
lemon wedges

Pound the marjoram leaves in a mortar and pestle with a little salt, or very finely chop them until they become a paste. Add the lemon juice, then stir in the olive oil and parsley, and season to taste.

Pull the leaves off the rosemary branches, leaving just a tuft at the end of each stem. Thread three pieces of fish and two scallops alternately onto each rosemary skewer, brush them with a little olive oil and season well.

Preheat the barbecue flat plate to medium direct heat. Cook the skewers for 3–4 minutes on each side or until the fish is cooked through. While the skewers are cooking, add the radicchio to the plate in batches for 1–2 minutes on each side or until it is just wilted and slightly browned. Put the radicchio wedges on a tray in a single layer so that the leaves don't steam in their own heat.

Arrange the radicchio on a flat serving dish, gently combine it with the rocket and drizzle a little of the marjoram dressing across the top. Serve the skewers with the radicchio salad, lemon wedges and the extra dressing.

Serves 4

Paprika lamb kebabs with skordalia

1 kg (2 lb 4 oz) lamb backstraps,
  cut into 2 cm (³/₄ inch) cubes
1 tablespoon sweet paprika
1 tablespoon hot paprika
125 ml (½ cup) lemon juice
125 ml (½ cup) olive oil
3 large (750 g/1 lb 10 oz) floury
  potatoes (e.g. russet), cut into
  large cubes
3–4 garlic cloves, crushed with a
  pinch of salt
300 g (10½ oz) English spinach
  leaves
lemon wedges, to serve

Thread six lamb cubes onto metallic skewers, then place in a non-metallic dish. Combine both the paprikas, 80 ml (⅓ cup) of lemon juice and 60 ml (¼ cup) of oil in a non-metallic jug. Pour over the skewers, turning to coat well. Season with pepper. Cover and chill while making the skordalia.

Boil the potatoes for 20 minutes, or until tender. Drain and place the potatoes, garlic and 1 tablespoon of the lemon juice in a food processor. With the motor running, slowly add the remaining oil in a thin stream and blend for 30–60 seconds, or until all the oil is incorporated — avoid overprocessing as it will become gluey. Season. Set aside to serve at room temperature.

Preheat a barboouc plate and brush with oil. Chargrill the skewers for 3–4 minutes each side for medium–rare, or 5–6 minutes for well done.

Wash the spinach and add to a saucepan with just the water clinging to the leaves. Cook, covered, over medium heat for 1–2 minutes, or until wilted. Remove from the heat and stir in the remaining lemon juice. Serve the kebabs immediately with the skordalia, spinach and lemon wedges.

Serves 4

Tuna skewers with Moroccan spices and chermoula

800 g (1 lb 12 oz) tuna steaks,
cut into cubes
2 tablespoons olive oil
½ teaspoon ground cumin
2 teaspoons grated lemon zest
couscous, to serve

Chermoula
3 teaspoons ground cumin
½ teaspoon ground coriander
2 teaspoons paprika
pinch of cayenne pepper
4 garlic cloves, crushed
15 g (½ cup) chopped flat-leaf
(Italian) parsley
30 g (½ cup) chopped coriander
(cilantro) leaves
80 ml (⅓ cup) lemon juice
125 ml (½ cup) olive oil

If using wooden skewers, soak for 30 minutes beforehand to prevent scorching. Place the tuna in a shallow non-metallic dish. Combine the olive oil, ground cumin and lemon zest and pour over the tuna. Toss to coat and leave to marinate for 10 minutes.

To make the chermoula, place the cumin, coriander, paprika and cayenne in a frying pan and cook over medium heat for 30 seconds, or until fragrant. Combine with the remaining ingredients and leave for the flavours to develop.

Thread the tuna onto the skewers. Cook on a hot, lightly oiled barbecue grill or flat plate until cooked to your taste (about 1 minute on each side for rare and 2 minutes for medium). Serve on couscous with the chermoula drizzled over the skewers.

Serves 4

Spice-rubbed pork kebabs with garlic sauce

800 g (1 lb 12 oz) pork neck fillet,
    trimmed
2 teaspoons fennel seeds
2 teaspoons coriander seeds
1 tablespoon olive oil

Garlic sauce
4 garlic cloves, coarsely chopped
1 thick slice of white bread, crusts
    removed
60 ml (¼ cup) olive oil
1½ tablespoons lemon juice

lemon wedges
pitta bread

Soak eight wooden skewers in cold water for 1 hour and cut the pork into 2 cm (¾ inch) cubes. Dry-fry the fennel and coriander seeds for about 30 seconds, or until they are fragrant, then grind them in a spice grinder or mortar and pestle. Mix the ground spices with the olive oil and toss the pork in it until the meat is well coated. Cover and refrigerate for 2 hours.

To make the garlic sauce, crush the garlic cloves in a mortar and pestle with ½ teaspoon salt until you have a very smooth paste. Tear the bread into pieces and leave it in a bowl with enough warm water to cover it. Let it soak for 5 minutes then squeeze out the bread and add it to the garlic, a little at a time, pounding as you go until you have a smooth paste. Keep pounding as you add the olive oil, 1 tablespoon at a time until it has all been added, then add 3 tablespoons of boiling water, one tablespoon at a time, and stir in the lemon juice. You should end up with a smooth, thick paste.

Thread the pork onto the soaked skewers and season the kebabs well with salt and ground pepper. Preheat the barbecue chargrill plate to medium–high direct heat and grill the kebabs for 10 minutes, or until they are cooked through, turning them halfway through the cooking time. Drizzle the kebabs with a little garlic sauce and put the rest of the sauce in a small bowl to serve at the table. Serve with the lemon wedges and warm pitta bread. The fennel salad (see page 309) makes a delicious accompaniment.

Serves 4

Note: You can also use a small food processor to make the garlic sauce. Beware! It has a very strong flavour, only a little is required.

Persian chicken skewers

2 teaspoons ground cardamom
½ teaspoon ground turmeric
1 teaspoon ground allspice
4 garlic cloves, crushed
60 ml (¼ cup) lemon juice
60 ml (¼ cup) olive oil
4 large chicken thigh fillets,
   excess fat removed
lemon wedges, to serve
plain yoghurt, to serve

To make the marinade, whisk together the cardamom, turmeric, allspice, garlic, lemon juice and oil. Season with salt and ground black pepper.

Cut each chicken thigh fillet into 3–4 cm (1¼–1½ inch) cubes. Toss the cubes in the spice marinade. Cover and refrigerate overnight.

Thread the chicken onto metal skewers and cook on a hot, lightly oiled barbecue grill or flat plate for 4 minutes on each side, or until the chicken is cooked through. Serve with lemon wedges and plain yoghurt.

Serves 4

Skewered lamb with chilli aïoli

1.5 kg (3 lb 5 oz) leg of lamb,
  boned and cubed
125 ml (½ cup) olive oil
125 ml (½ cup) lemon juice
2 garlic cloves, crushed
1 teaspoon cracked black pepper
1 tablespoon Dijon mustard
1 tablespoon chopped oregano

Chilli aïoli
2–3 small red chillies, seeded
3 garlic cloves
½ teaspoon ground black pepper
3 egg yolks
2 tablespoons lemon juice
200 ml (7 fl oz) olive oil

Put the lamb in a large, non-metallic bowl. Add the combined olive oil, lemon juice, garlic, pepper, mustard and oregano. Toss well, cover and refrigerate for at least 3 hours.

Soak 12 wooden skewers in water to prevent scorching. Drain the lamb, reserving the marinade. Thread the lamb onto the skewers and cook on a hot, lightly oiled barbecue grill or flat plate until well browned, brushing with the marinade occasionally.

To make the chilli aïoli, chop the chillies and garlic for 30 seconds in a food processor. Add the pepper, egg yolks and 2 teaspoons of lemon juice. With the motor running, slowly pour in the oil in a fine stream. Increase the flow as the aïoli thickens. Add the remaining lemon juice and season to taste. Serve with the skewered lamb.

Makes 12 skewers

Mushroom and eggplant skewers with tomato sauce

12 long rosemary sprigs
18 Swiss brown mushrooms, halved
1 small eggplant (aubergine), cubed
60 ml (¼ cup) olive oil
2 tablespoons balsamic vinegar
2 garlic cloves, crushed
1 teaspoon sugar

Tomato sauce
5 tomatoes
1 tablespoon olive oil
1 small onion, finely chopped
1 garlic clove, crushed
1 tablespoon tomato paste (purée)
2 teaspoons sugar
2 teaspoons balsamic vinegar
1 tablespoon chopped flat-leaf
   (Italian) parsley

Remove the leaves from the lower part of the rosemary sprigs. Reserve 1 tablespoon of the leaves. Put the mushrooms and eggplant in a large non-metallic bowl. Pour on the combined oil, vinegar, garlic and sugar and toss. Marinate for about 15 minutes.

To make the tomato sauce, score a cross in the base of each tomato. Put in a bowl of boiling water for 30 seconds, then plunge into cold water. Peel the skin away from the cross. Cut in half and scoop out the seeds with a teaspoon. Dice the flesh.

Heat the oil in a saucepan. Cook the onion and garlic over medium heat for 2–3 minutes, or until soft. Reduce the heat, add the tomato, tomato paste, sugar, vinegar and parsley and simmer for 10 minutes, or until thick.

Carefully thread alternating mushroom halves and eggplant cubes onto the rosemary sprigs. Cook on a hot, lightly oiled barbecue grill or flat plate for 7–8 minutes, or until the eggplant is tender, turning occasionally. Serve with the sauce.

Serves 4

Vegetarian skewers with basil couscous

5 thin zucchini (courgettes), cut into
  2 cm (³/₄ inch) cubes
5 slender eggplants (aubergines),
  cut into 2 cm (³/₄ inch) cubes
12 button mushrooms, halved
2 red capsicums (peppers), cut into
  2 cm (³/₄ inch) cubes
250 g (9 oz) kefalotyri cheese, cut
  into 2 cm (³/₄ inch) thick pieces
80 ml (¹/₃ cup) lemon juice
2 garlic cloves, finely chopped
5 tablespoons finely chopped basil
145 ml (5 fl oz) extra virgin olive oil
185 g (1 cup) couscous
1 teaspoon grated lemon zest
lemon wedges, to serve

Using 12 metallic skewers, thread alternate pieces of vegetables and kefalotyri, starting and finishing with capsicum and using two pieces of kefalotyri per skewer. Place in a large non-metallic dish. Combine the lemon juice, garlic, 4 tablespoons of basil and 125 ml (½ cup) of oil in a non-metallic bowl. Season. Pour two-thirds of the marinade over the skewers, reserving the remainder. Turn the skewers to coat evenly, cover with plastic wrap and marinate for at least 5 minutes.

Put the couscous, zest and 375 ml (1½ cups) boiling water in a large heatproof bowl. Stand for 5 minutes, or until the water has been absorbed. Add the remaining oil and basil, then fluff with a fork to separate the grains.

Meanwhile, heat a barbecue plate to medium–high. Cook the skewers, brushing often with the leftover marinade, for 4–5 minutes each side, or until the vegetables are cooked and the cheese browns.

Divide the couscous and skewers among four serving plates. Season, then drizzle with the reserved marinade. Serve immediately with lemon wedges.

Serves 4

Salmon and prawn kebabs with chinese spices

4 x 200 g (7 oz) salmon fillets
36 raw prawns (shrimp), peeled,
  deveined, tails intact
5 cm (2 inch) piece fresh ginger,
  finely shredded
170 ml (²/₃ cup) Chinese rice wine
185 ml (³/₄ cup) kecap manis
¹/₂ teaspoon five-spice powder
200 g (7 oz) fresh egg noodles
600 g (1 lb 5 oz) baby bok choy
  (pak choi), leaves separated

Remove the skin and bones from the salmon and cut it into bite-sized cubes (you should have about 36). Thread three cubes of salmon alternately with three prawns onto each skewer. Lay the skewers in a non-metallic dish.

Mix together the ginger, rice wine, kecap manis and five-spice powder. Pour over the skewers, then cover and marinate for at least 2 hours. Turn over a few times to ensure even coating.

Drain, reserving the marinade. Cook the skewers in batches on a hot, lightly oiled barbecue flat plate or grill for 4–5 minutes each side, or until they are cooked through.

Meanwhile, place the noodles in a bowl and cover with boiling water. Leave for 5 minutes, or until tender, then drain and keep warm. Place the reserved marinade in a saucepan and bring to the boil. Reduce the heat, simmer and stir in the bok choy leaves. Cook, covered, for 2 minutes, or until just wilted.

Top the noodles with the bok choy, then the kebabs. Spoon on the heated marinade, season and serve.

Serves 4

Mediterranean chicken skewers

2 large chicken breast fillets, cut
  into 32 cubes
24 cherry tomatoes
6 cap mushrooms, cut into quarters
2 garlic cloves, crushed
zest of 1 lemon, grated
2 tablespoons lemon juice
2 tablespoons olive oil
1 tablespoon oregano leaves,
  chopped

Soak eight wooden skewers in water to prevent scorching. Thread a piece of chicken onto each skewer, followed by a tomato, then a piece of mushroom. Repeat twice for each skewer and finish with a piece of chicken. Put the skewers in a shallow, non-metallic dish.

Combine the garlic, lemon zest, lemon juice, olive oil and chopped oregano, pour over the skewers and toss well. Marinate for at least 2 hours, or overnight if time permits.

Cook the skewers on a hot, lightly oiled barbecue grill or flat plate for 4 minutes on each side, basting occasionally, until the chicken is cooked and the tomatoes have shrivelled slightly.

Makes 8 skewers

Burgers

Chilli beef burgers

500 g (1 lb 2 oz) minced (ground) beef
6 red Asian shallots, finely chopped
25 g (¼ cup) crisp fried onion flakes
  (see Note)
3 garlic cloves, finely chopped
2 long red chillies, seeded and finely
  chopped
20 g (⅓ cup) finely chopped coriander
  (cilantro) leaves (include some
  stems)
2–2½ tablespoons chilli garlic sauce
  (see Note)
1 egg, lightly beaten
160 g (2 cups) fresh breadcrumbs

olive oil, for brushing
1 loaf Turkish bread, cut into 4 pieces,
  or 4 round Turkish rolls
100 g (3 handfuls) mignonette or
  green oak lettuce leaves

To make the burgers, put the beef, shallots, onion flakes, garlic, chilli, coriander, chilli garlic sauce, egg, breadcrumbs and 1½ teaspoons of salt in a large bowl, and knead well with your hands until the ingredients are thoroughly combined. Cover the bowl and refrigerate for 2 hours.

Using wet hands, divide the beef mixture into four equal portions, roll each portion into a ball, then flatten it slightly to form patties. Preheat the chargrill plate to medium direct heat. Brush the patties lightly with oil and grill them for 5–6 minutes, then flip them over and cook for another 5–6 minutes, or until they are well browned and cooked through. A few minutes before the patties are done, toast the bread, cut-side down, on the chargrill plate for 1–2 minutes, or until it is marked and golden.

Divide the lettuce among four of the toasted bread slices. Add a patty, season the burgers with salt and pepper, then top with the remaining toasted bread. Delicious served with pineapple mint salsa (see page 318).

Serves 4

Note: Crisp fried onion flakes and chilli garlic sauce are available from Asian grocery stores.

Tuna burgers with herbed mayonnaise

4 garlic cloves, crushed
2 egg yolks
250 ml (1 cup) light olive oil
3 tablespoons chopped flat-leaf
  (Italian) parsley
1 tablespoon chopped dill
2 teaspoons Dijon mustard
1 tablespoon lemon juice
1 tablespoon red wine vinegar
1 tablespoon baby capers in brine,
  drained
4 anchovy fillets in oil, drained
4 x 150 g (5½ oz) tuna steaks
2 tablespoons olive oil
2 red onions, thinly sliced
4 large round bread rolls, halved
  and buttered
100 g (3½ oz) mixed lettuce
  leaves

Put the garlic and egg yolks in a food processor and process them together for 10 seconds. With the motor running, add the oil in a very thin, slow stream. When the mixture starts to thicken start pouring the oil a little faster until all of the oil has been added and the mixture is thick and creamy. Add the parsley, dill, mustard, lemon juice, vinegar, capers and anchovies, and process until the mixture is smooth. Refrigerate the mayonnaise until you need it.

Preheat the chargrill plate to high direct heat. Brush the tuna steaks with 1 tablespoon of olive oil and cook them for 2 minutes on each side, or until they are almost cooked through. Add the remaining olive oil to the onion, toss to separate and coat the rings, and cook on the flat plate for 2 minutes, or until the onion is soft and caramelized. Toast the rolls, buttered-side down, on the chargrill plate for 1 minute, or until they are marked and golden.

Put some lettuce, a tuna steak, some of the onion and a dollop of herbed mayonnaise on one half of each roll. Season with salt and pepper and top with the other half of the roll.

Serves 4

Pork and tomato burgers

350 g (12 oz) minced (ground) pork
and veal
100 g (3½ oz) sun-dried tomatoes,
chopped
3 spring onions (scallions), finely
chopped
2 tablespoons chopped basil
1 red capsicum (pepper), seeded
and sliced
olive oil, for cooking
1 tablespoon balsamic vinegar

Mix together the pork and veal, sun-dried tomato, spring onion and basil. Season well and knead for 2 minutes, or until a little sticky. Form into four burgers and refrigerate for at least 15 minutes.

Mix the capsicum with a little olive oil. Cook on a hot, lightly oiled barbecue grill or flat plate, tossing well and drizzling with the balsamic vinegar, until just softened. Set aside.

Wipe the barbecue clean and reheat. Brush the burgers with a little olive oil and cook for 4–5 minutes each side, or until browned and cooked through. Serve with the chargrilled capsicum.

Serves 4

Yakitori chicken burgers

4 chicken thigh fillets, trimmed
185 ml (¾ cup) yakitori sauce
1 teaspoon cornflour (cornstarch)
oil, for brushing
4 soft hamburger buns, halved
80 g (⅓ cup) Japanese mayonnaise
(see Note)
80 g (2 handfuls) mizuna lettuce
1 Lebanese (short) cucumber, ends
trimmed and shaved into ribbons
with a vegetable peeler

Toss the chicken and yakitori sauce together in a bowl until the chicken fillets are well coated, then cover and refrigerate for 4 hours.

Drain the yakitori sauce from the chicken into a small saucepan and sprinkle it with the cornflour. Stir the cornflour into the marinade, bring the mixture to the boil and simmer, stirring frequently, for 5 minutes, or until it is thickened, then keep it warm.

Lightly brush the chargrill with oil, preheat it to low–medium direct heat and cook the chicken on the chargrill for 6–7 minutes on each side, or until it is cooked through. Toast the burger buns for about 1 minute on each side, or until they are marked and golden.

Spread some mayonnaise on the inside surface of each bun, cover the base with mizuna and cucumber ribbons, and top with the chicken. Spread some of the thickened marinade over the chicken and top with the other half of the bun.

Serves 4

Note: Japanese mayonnaise will be available in larger supermarkets and Asian speciality stores. If you can't find it, use regular whole-egg mayonnaise instead.

Beef and mozzarella burgers with chargrilled tomatoes

500 g (1 lb 2 oz) minced (ground) beef
160 g (2 cups) fresh breadcrumbs
1 small red onion, very finely chopped
4 garlic cloves, crushed
30 g (½ cup) finely shredded basil
  leaves
50 g (1¾ oz) pitted black olives,
  finely chopped
1 tablespoon balsamic vinegar
1 egg
8 pieces mozzarella 2 cm x 3 cm x
  5 mm (¾ x 1¼ x ¼ inch)
olive oil spray

Chargrilled tomatoes
6 Roma (plum) tomatoes
1½ tablespoons olive oil

Put the beef, breadcrumbs, onion, garlic, basil, olives, balsamic vinegar and egg in a large bowl and season well with salt and pepper. Use your hands to mix it all together, then cover and refrigerate the mixture for about 2 hours.

Divide the beef mixture into eight portions and roll each portion into a ball. Push a piece of mozzarella into the middle of each ball, then push the mince mixture over to cover the hole and flatten the ball to form a patty.

To make the chargrilled tomatoes, slice the tomatoes in half lengthways and toss them with the olive oil. Spray the flat plate with olive oil and preheat it to high direct heat. Cook the tomatoes, cut-side down, for 8 minutes then turn them over and cook for another 5 minutes or until they are soft.

Cook the patties on one side for 5 minutes then flip them and cook for another 5 minutes or until they are completely cooked through and the cheese has melted. Serve the burgers and chargrilled tomatoes with a fresh green salad.

Serves 4

Pork sausage burgers with mustard cream

800 g (1 lb 12 oz) minced (ground)
  pork
1 small onion, finely chopped
80 g (1 cup) fresh breadcrumbs
2 garlic cloves, crushed
1 egg, lightly beaten
1 teaspoon dried sage
6 long bread rolls

Mustard cream
125 g (½ cup) sour cream
1 tablespoon wholegrain mustard
2 teaspoons lemon juice

Mix together the pork, onion, breadcrumbs, garlic, egg and sage with your hands. Season well. Divide the mixture into six portions and shape into sausages.

Cook the sausages on a hot, lightly oiled barbecue flat plate or grill for 5–10 minutes, turning occasionally.

To make the mustard cream, put the sour cream, mustard and juice in a small bowl and stir together. Spread each cut side of the rolls with a little mustard cream, then sandwich the sausage burgers in the middle. Serve with the remaining mustard cream.

Serves 6

Lamb burger

1 tablespoon ground cumin
250 g (1 cup) plain Greek-style
  yoghurt
½ Lebanese (short) cucumber,
  grated
1 tablespoon finely chopped mint
  leaves
1 tablespoon olive oil
1 onion, finely chopped
2 garlic cloves, crushed
800 g (1 lb 12 oz) minced (ground)
  lamb
2 tablespoons finely chopped
  flat-leaf (Italian) parsley
2 tablespoons finely chopped
  coriander (cilantro) leaves
2 red capsicums (peppers),
  quartered and seeded
1 tablespoon olive oil, extra
2 red onions, thinly sliced
olive oil spray
1 loaf Turkish bread, cut into 4 pieces
  and split horizontally
100 g (3½ oz) baby rocket (arugula)
  leaves

Dry-fry 1 teaspoon ground cumin over medium heat for 30 seconds, or until it is fragrant. Put the yoghurt, cucumber, mint and dry-fried cumin in a small bowl and mix it all together. Cover the bowl and refrigerate it until needed.

Heat the oil in a frying pan and cook the onion over medium heat for 2–3 minutes or until softened. Add the garlic and remaining cumin, cook it for another minute, then allow the mixture to cool. Put the onion mixture in a large bowl with the lamb, parsley and coriander, season with salt and pepper and mix it together with your hands. Divide the mixture into four portions, and shape each portion into a 2 cm (¾ inch) thick patty.

Heat the barbecue to medium–high direct heat. Toss the capsicum with the extra oil and cook it on the flat plate for 6 minutes on each side or until it is softened and lightly charred. Grill the patties on the flat plate for 5–6 minutes each side or until they are done.

Spray the red onion with the olive oil spray and cook it on the flat plate for 2–3 minutes or until soft and golden. Toast the bread, cut-side down, on the chargrill plate for 1–2 minutes or until it is marked and golden.

To assemble the burgers, put some rocket on four of the bread slices. Put a patty on top, then the capsicum and onion. Dollop 2–3 tablespoons of the yoghurt mixture on each and season with salt and freshly ground black pepper. Top with the remaining bread slices and serve them straight away.

Serves 4

Steak sandwich with balsamic onions and sun-dried tomato and basil cream

125 g (½ cup) sour cream
40 g (1½ oz) sun-dried tomatoes,
  well drained and finely chopped
3 garlic cloves, crushed
2 tablespoons finely chopped
  basil leaves
2 teaspoons lemon juice
2 red onions
2 tablespoons olive oil
2 tablespoons balsamic vinegar
1 tablespoon soft brown sugar
8 large slices of sourdough bread
400 g (14 oz) piece of fillet steak,
  cut into 1 cm (½ inch) thick slices
55 g (2 oz) baby rocket (arugula)
  leaves, rinsed and well drained

Preheat the barbecue to medium–high direct heat. Mix the sour cream, sun-dried tomatoes, garlic, basil and lemon juice in a small bowl and season the mixture to taste.

Thinly slice the onions, separate the rings and toss them with 1 tablespoon of olive oil. Spread the onion across the flat grill plate and cook it for 10 minutes, or until softened and starting to brown. Gather the rings into a pile and pour the combined balsamic vinegar and sugar over them. Turn the onion so that it is well coated in the balsamic mixture, then spread it out a little and cook for a few more minutes, or until it is slightly glazed. Remove the onion from the barbecue and toast the bread on the chargrill plate for 30 seconds on each side, or until grill marks appear.

Brush the steaks with a little olive oil and season with salt and ground black pepper. Chargrill them for 1 minute each side for medium–rare, or 2 minutes for well done.

To serve, put a piece of steak on a slice of toasted bread and top with the onion, a dollop of the sour cream mixture and some rocket leaves. Finish with a second piece of toast.

Serves 4

Vegetarian burgers with coriander garlic cream

250 g (1 cup) red lentils
1 tablespoon oil
2 onions, sliced
1 tablespoon tandoori mix powder
425 g (15 oz) tin chickpeas, drained
1 tablespoon grated fresh ginger
1 egg
3 tablespoons chopped flat-leaf
  (Italian) parsley
2 tablespoons chopped coriander
  (cilantro) leaves
180 g (2¼ cups) fresh breadcrumbs
plain (all-purpose) flour, for dusting

Coriander garlic cream
125 g (½ cup) sour cream
125 ml (½ cup) cream
1 garlic clove, crushed
2 tablespoons chopped coriander
  (cilantro) leaves
2 tablespoons chopped flat-leaf
  (Italian) parsley

Simmer the lentils in a large pan of water for 8 minutes or until tender. Drain well. Heat the oil in a pan and cook the onion until tender. Add the tandoori mix and stir until fragrant.

Put the chickpeas, half the lentils, the ginger, egg and onion mixture in a food processor. Process for 20 seconds or until smooth. Transfer to a bowl. Stir in the remaining lentils, parsley, coriander and breadcrumbs.

Divide into 10 portions and shape into burgers (if the mixture is too soft, refrigerate for 15 minutes to firm). Toss the burgers in flour and place on a hot, lightly oiled barbecue grill or flat plate. Cook for 3–4 minutes each side or until browned.

For the coriander garlic cream, mix together the sour cream, cream, garlic and herbs. Serve with the burgers.

Makes 10 burgers

Cheeseburgers with capsicum salsa

Capsicum salsa
2 red capsicums (peppers)
1 ripe tomato, finely chopped
1 small red onion, finely chopped
1 tablespoon olive oil
2 teaspoons red wine vinegar

1 kg (2 lb 4 oz) minced (ground)
  beef
1 small onion, finely chopped
2 tablespoons chopped flat-leaf
  (Italian) parsley
1 teaspoon dried oregano
1 tablespoon tomato paste (purée)
70 g (2½ oz) Cheddar cheese
6 bread rolls
salad leaves, to serve

To make the salsa, quarter the capsicums, remove the seeds and membranes and cook on a hot, lightly oiled barbecue grill, skin-side down, until the skin blackens and blisters. Place in a plastic bag and leave to cool. Peel away the skin and dice the flesh. Combine with the tomato, onion, olive oil and vinegar and leave for at least 1 hour to let the flavours develop. Serve at room temperature.

Mix together the ground beef, onion, herbs and tomato paste with your hands and season well. Divide into six portions and shape into six patties. Cut the cheese into small squares. Make a cavity in the top of each patty with your thumb. Place a piece of cheese in the cavity and smooth the mince over to enclose the cheese completely.

Cook the patties on a hot, lightly oiled barbecue grill or flat plate for 4–5 minutes each side, turning once. Serve in rolls with salad leaves and capsicum salsa.

Serves 6

Note: As a variation, try using Camembert, Brie or any blue cheese instead of the Cheddar.

Herb burgers

750 g (1 lb 10 oz) minced (ground)
  lamb
2 tablespoons chopped basil
1 tablespoon chopped chives
1 tablespoon chopped rosemary
1 tablespoon chopped thyme
2 tablespoons lemon juice
80 g (1 cup) fresh breadcrumbs
1 egg
2 long crusty bread sticks
lettuce leaves, rinsed and dried
2 tomatoes, sliced
tomato sauce, to serve

Combine the lamb with the herbs, juice, breadcrumbs, egg and season well with salt and pepper. Mix well with your hands. Divide the mixture into eight portions and shape into thick rectangular patties.

Place the burgers on a hot, lightly oiled barbecue grill or flat plate. Cook for 5–10 minutes each side until well browned and just cooked through.

Cut the bread sticks in half and sandwich with the burgers, lettuce, tomato and tomato sauce.

Makes 8 burgers

Brunch burger with the works

750 g (1 lb 10 oz) minced (ground)
    beef
1 onion, finely chopped
1 egg
40 g (½ cup) fresh breadcrumbs
2 tablespoons tomato paste (purée)
1 tablespoon Worcestershire sauce
2 tablespoons chopped flat-leaf
    (Italian) parsley
3 large onions
30 g (1 oz) butter
6 slices Cheddar cheese
butter, extra, for cooking
6 eggs, extra
6 rashers bacon
6 large hamburger buns, lightly
    toasted
shredded lettuce
2 tomatoes, thinly sliced
6 large slices beetroot, drained
6 pineapple rings, drained
tomato sauce, to serve

Mix together the beef, onion, egg, breadcrumbs, tomato paste, Worcestershire sauce and parsley with your hands. Season well. Divide into six portions and shape into burgers. Cover and set aside.

Slice the onions into thin rings. Heat the butter on a barbecue flat plate. Cook the onion, turning often, until well browned. Move the onion to the outer edge of the flat plate to keep warm. Brush the barbecue grill or flat plate liberally with oil.

Cook the burgers for 3–4 minutes each side or until browned and cooked through. Move to the cooler part of the barbecue or transfer to a plate and keep warm. Place a slice of cheese on each burger.

Heat a small amount of butter on a barbecue flat plate or in a large frying pan. Fry the eggs and bacon until the eggs are cooked through and the bacon is golden and crisp. Fill the hamburger buns with lettuce, tomato, beetroot and pineapple topped with a burger. Pile the onion, egg, bacon and tomato sauce on top of the burger.

Serves 6

Mains

Swordfish with tomato butter and grilled asparagus

100 g (3½ oz) butter, softened
50 g (⅓ cup) semi-dried (sun-blushed) tomatoes, finely chopped
2 tablespoons baby capers in brine, drained and crushed
1½ tablespoons shredded basil leaves
4 garlic cloves, crushed
60 ml (¼ cup) extra virgin olive oil
300 g (10½ oz) slender asparagus spears, trimmed
4 swordfish steaks

Put the butter in a bowl with the tomato, capers, basil and two cloves of crushed garlic, and mash it all together. Shape the flavoured butter into a log, then wrap it in baking paper and twist the ends to close them off. Refrigerate until the butter is firm, then cut it into 1 cm (½ inch) slices and leave it, covered, at room temperature until needed.

Mix 2 tablespoons of the oil and the remaining garlic in a small bowl. Toss the asparagus spears with the oil until they are well coated, season them with salt and pepper, and leave for 30 minutes.

Preheat a ridged barbecue grill plate to high direct heat. Brush the swordfish steaks with the remaining oil and cook them for 2–3 minutes on each side or until they are just cooked through. Don't overcook the fish as residual heat will continue to cook the meat after it has been removed from the barbecue. Put a piece of the tomato butter on top of each steak as soon as it comes off the barbecue and season to taste. Cook the asparagus on the chargrill plate, turning it regularly, for 2–3 minutes, or until it is just tender. Serve the asparagus immediately with the fish.

Serves 4

Sage and ricotta stuffed chicken

250 g (1 cup) fresh ricotta cheese, well drained
1 tablespoon shredded sage leaves
2 garlic cloves, crushed
1½ teaspoons grated lemon zest
40 g (1½ oz) finely grated Parmesan cheese
4 chicken breast fillets, tenderloin removed
8 thin slices prosciutto
olive oil, for brushing

Mix together the ricotta, sage, garlic, zest and Parmesan until they are well combined. Use a sharp knife to cut a large pocket into the side of each chicken breast and fill each pocket with a quarter of the ricotta mixture. Pin the pockets closed with toothpicks and wrap each breast in two slices of prosciutto, securing it with a toothpick.

Heat a barbecue flat plate to medium direct heat, brush the chicken parcels with olive oil and season them with freshly ground black pepper. Cook them for 8 minutes on each side, or until they are cooked through. This is delicious served with baby spinach salad (see page 338).

Serves 4

Greek pepper lamb salad

300 g (10½ oz) lamb backstraps
1½ tablespoons cracked black
  pepper
3 vine-ripened tomatoes, cut into
  8 wedges
2 Lebanese (short) cucumbers, sliced
150 g (5½ oz) lemon and garlic
  marinated Kalamata olives, drained
  (reserving 1½ tablespoons oil)
100 g (3½ oz) Greek feta, cubed
¾ teaspoon dried oregano
1 tablespoon lemon juice
1 tablespoon extra virgin olive oil

Roll the backstraps in the pepper, pressing the pepper on with your fingers. Cover and refrigerate for about 15 minutes. Place the tomato, cucumber, olives, feta and ½ teaspoon of the dried oregano in a bowl.

Heat a chargrill pan or barbecue plate, brush with oil and when very hot, cook the lamb for 2–3 minutes on each side, or until cooked to your liking. Keep warm.

Whisk the lemon juice, extra virgin olive oil, reserved Kalamata oil and the remaining dried oregano together well. Season. Pour half the dressing over the salad, toss together and arrange on a serving platter.

Cut the lamb on the diagonal into 1 cm (½ inch) thick slices and arrange on top of the salad. Pour the rest of the dressing on top and serve.

Serves 4

Moroccan pumpkin on pistachio couscous

1 kg (2 lb 4 oz) pumpkin
2 tablespoons olive oil
250 ml (1 cup) vegetable stock
185 g (1 cup) instant couscous
250 g (1 cup) plain Greek-style
  yoghurt
1 tablespoon lemon juice
1 tablespoon honey
1 tablespoon butter
2 garlic cloves, crushed
1 small onion, finely diced
2 tablespoons finely chopped
  flat-leaf (Italian) parsley
2 tablespoons finely chopped
  coriander (cilantro) leaves
35 g (¼ cup) roasted, shelled and
  roughly chopped pistachio nuts
2 tablespoons ras el hanout or
  Moroccan spice blend (see Note)

Peel the pumpkin, cut it into 2 cm (¾ inch) thick pieces and toss it in a bowl with the olive oil and remaining spice mix. Preheat a covered or kettle barbecue to medium direct heat. Grill the pumpkin, covered, for 45 minutes, or until it is golden all over and cooked through.

Bring the vegetable stock to the boil, pour it over the couscous and stir to combine them. Cover the bowl with plastic wrap and leave it for 10 minutes, or until all of the stock has been absorbed.

Spoon the yoghurt into a small bowl, stir in the lemon juice and honey, and season to taste.

Melt the butter in a small frying pan, add the garlic and onion and cook them over low heat for 5 minutes, or until they are softened. Add the onion mixture to the couscous with the parsley, coriander, pistachio nuts and 2 teaspoons of the spice mix, stir it together and season to taste.

Pile the couscous onto a serving plate, top it with the grilled pumpkin pieces and serve with the yoghurt dressing.

Serves 4–6

Note: Ras el hanout is a traditional Moroccan spice mix, and is available from gourmet food stores. The taste of this dish will rely on the quality of the spices used, so if you have time, make your own. Dry-fry 6 cardamom pods, ½ teaspoon black pepper and 1 teaspoon fennel seeds until they are fragrant. Let the spices cool, then grind them in a spice grinder or mortar and pestle and mix with ½ teaspoon ground cinnamon, 1 teaspoon turmeric, ½ teaspoon cayenne pepper, 2 teaspoons mild paprika, 1 teaspoon ground cumin, ½ teaspoon allspice and 1 teaspoon salt. The spice mix can be stored in an airtight container for up to 2 months.

Chicken salad with rocket and cannellini beans

80 ml (⅓ cup) lemon juice
3 garlic cloves, crushed
1 teaspoon soft brown sugar
15 g (¼ cup) finely chopped basil
125 ml (½ cup) olive oil
4 chicken breast fillets
400 g (14 oz) tin cannellini beans,
  rinsed and drained
100 g (3½ oz) small rocket (arugula)
  leaves

Whisk together the lemon juice, garlic, sugar, basil and olive oil, and season lightly with salt and pepper. Pour a third of the dressing over the chicken to coat. Cook the chicken on a hot, lightly oiled barbecue grill or flat plate for 4 minutes on each side, or until cooked through.

Meanwhile, combine the beans and rocket with the remaining dressing, toss well and season. Slice the chicken and serve over the rocket and beans.

Serves 4

Chipolatas with cheese and jalapeño quesadillas

2 tablespoons olive oil
2 garlic cloves, crushed
2 x 400 g (14 oz) tins crushed
   tomatoes
½ teaspoon ground cumin
16 x 15 cm (6 inch) flour tortillas
320 g (11½ oz) coarsely grated
   Cheddar cheese
60 g (⅓ cup) pickled jalapeño chillies,
   drained and roughly chopped
20 spicy chipolatas
coriander (cilantro) sprigs

Heat the olive oil in a frying pan over medium heat and cook the garlic for 1–2 minutes or until it is just beginning to turn golden. Add the crushed tomatoes and cumin, and season well. Reduce the heat to low and cook the relish for 30–35 minutes or until it becomes thick and pulpy.

In the meantime, sprinkle a tortilla with 40 g (⅓ cup) of the grated cheese, leaving a 1 cm (½ inch) border around the edge. Scatter 1½ teaspoons of the jalapeño chillies over the cheese and put another tortilla on top, pressing it down. Repeat the process with the remaining tortillas, cheese and jalapeños to make eight quesadillas.

Preheat the barbecue to low direct heat. Cook the chipolatas on the flat plate, turning them occasionally, for 10–12 minutes or until they are cooked through. When the chipolatas are nearly ready, start cooking the quesadillas on the chargrill for 1–2 minutes on each side, or until the cheese has melted. You may need to do this in batches, so make sure you keep them warm as you go. Cut each quesadilla into quarters and serve with the tomato relish and chipolatas. Garnish with the coriander.

Serves 4

Vietnamese fish

750 g (1 lb 10 oz) small, firm
  white fish
2 teaspoons green peppercorns,
  finely crushed
2 teaspoons chopped red chilli
3 teaspoons fish sauce
2 teaspoons oil
1 tablespoon oil, extra
2 onions, finely sliced
4 cm (1 ½ inch) piece fresh ginger,
  peeled and thinly sliced
3 garlic cloves, finely sliced
2 teaspoons sugar
4 spring onions (scallions), cut into
  short lengths, then finely shredded

Lemon and garlic dipping sauce
3 tablespoons lemon juice
2 tablespoons fish sauce
1 tablespoon sugar
2 small red chillies, chopped
3 garlic cloves, crushed

Cut 2 diagonal slashes in the thickest part of the fish on both sides. In a food processor or mortar and pestle, grind the peppercorns, chilli and fish sauce to a paste and brush over the fish. Leave for 20 minutes.

To make the dipping sauce, mix together all the ingredients.

Cook the fish on a hot, lightly oiled barbecue grill or flat plate for 8 minutes on each side, or until the flesh flakes easily when tested.

While the fish is cooking, heat the extra oil in a pan and stir the onion over medium heat, until golden. Add the ginger, garlic and sugar and cook for 3 minutes. Place the fish on a serving plate, top with the onion mixture and sprinkle with spring onion. Serve with the dipping sauce.

Serves 6

Coriander prawns

8 very large raw prawns (shrimp)
1 tablespoon sweet chilli sauce
1 teaspoon ground coriander
125 ml (½ cup) olive oil
80 ml (⅓ cup) lime juice
3 garlic cloves, crushed
1 tomato, peeled, seeded and
   chopped
2 tablespoons roughly chopped
   coriander (cilantro)

Remove the heads from the prawns
and, with a sharp knife, cut the
prawns in half lengthways, leaving the
tails attached. Pull out each dark vein.

Mix together the sweet chilli sauce
and ground coriander with half the
olive oil, half the lime juice and half the
garlic. Add the prawns, toss to coat,
then cover and marinate in the fridge
for 30 minutes.

Meanwhile, to make the dressing, mix
the remaining olive oil, lime juice and
garlic in a bowl with the chopped
tomato and coriander.

Drain the prawns, reserving the
marinade and cook, cut-side down,
on a hot, lightly oiled barbecue grill or
flat plate for 1–2 minutes each side,
or until cooked through, brushing
occasionally with the marinade.
Spoon a little of the dressing over
the prawns and season well with
salt and pepper before serving.

Serves 4

Marinated lamb cutlets with orange sweet potatoes and ginger nori butter

16 lamb cutlets
125 ml (½ cup) Japanese plum wine
  (see Note)
2 tablespoons Japanese soy sauce
1 teaspoon finely grated fresh ginger
2 garlic cloves, crushed
few drops sesame oil
4 x 200 g (7 oz) orange sweet
  potatoes
oil, for brushing

Ginger nori butter
90 g (3¼ oz) butter, softened
1½ tablespoons very finely shredded
  nori
2 teaspoons finely grated fresh
  ginger

Trim the lamb cutlets of any excess fat. Mix together the plum wine, soy sauce, grated ginger, garlic and sesame oil, add the cutlets to the marinade and turn them a few times so they are well coated. Cover the dish with plastic wrap and refrigerate it for 3 hours.

To make the ginger nori butter, mash the butter, shredded nori and grated ginger together and season to taste with pepper.

Preheat a covered barbecue to medium indirect heat. Brush the sweet potatoes with a little oil and wrap in a double layer of foil. Put them on the barbecue and replace the lid. Roast the potatoes for 50 minutes, or until they are tender when pierced with a sharp knife, then remove them from the heat and leave the barbecue uncovered.

Drain the marinade into a small saucepan and boil it over high heat for 5 minutes or until it is reduced by about half. Brush the chargrill plate with a little oil and cook the cutlets for 1 minute, then turn them over, brush with the reduced marinade and cook them for another minute. This will give a rare cutlet, so if you like your meat cooked a little more, you'll need to extend the cooking time on each side

by a minute or so. Remove the cutlets from the barbecue, brush them with the remaining reduced marinade, cover, and leave them to rest for 3 minutes. Serve the lamb with the orange sweet potatoes topped with nori butter. They are delicious with an Asian leaf salad (try a few handfuls each of mizuna, baby tatsoi and Chinese cabbage) or lightly steamed Asian greens.

Serves 4

Note: Japanese plum wine is available from specialist Japanese grocery stores and some liquor suppliers.

Chicken tikka with garlic naan and apple raita

100 g (⅓ cup) tikka paste
60 g (¼ cup) thick yoghurt
600 g (1 lb 5 oz) chicken breast fillet,
    cut into 3 cm (1¼ inch) cubes
2 small red onions, quartered
oil, for brushing
2 tablespoons chopped coriander
    (cilantro) leaves

Apple raita
1 green apple, grated
2 teaspoons lemon juice
60 g (¼ cup) sour cream
3 tablespoons chopped mint leaves

Garlic naan
1 garlic clove, crushed
2 tablespoons butter, softened
4 plain naan bread

Stir the tikka paste and yoghurt together, add the chicken and turn it until it is evenly coated in the tikka mixture. Cover the chicken with plastic wrap and refrigerate it for 4 hours or overnight.

To make the raita, put the grated apple, lemon juice, sour cream and mint in a small bowl and stir it all together. Cover the bowl and refrigerate it until you are ready to dish up. Mash the crushed garlic and butter together and brush one side of each piece of naan with about 2 teaspoons of garlic butter.

Soak four wooden skewers in cold water for 1 hour and preheat the barbecue to low–medium direct heat. Thread the chicken and onion pieces onto the skewers and cook them on the flat plate for 5–6 minutes on each side, turning once. A little before the chicken is ready, lightly brush the chargrill plate with some oil. Grill the naan, buttered-side down, for 1–2 minutes, or until the bread is golden and marked. Turn it and grill for another minute on the other side.

Sprinkle the skewers with the chopped coriander and serve them with the garlic naan and apple raita.

Serves 4

Pepper steaks with horseradish sauce

4 sirloin steaks
3 tablespoons seasoned cracked
  pepper

Horseradish sauce
2 tablespoons brandy
3 tablespoons beef stock
4 tablespoons cream
1 tablespoon horseradish cream
1/2 teaspoon sugar

Coat the steaks on both sides with pepper, pressing it into the meat. Cook on a hot, lightly oiled barbecue grill or flat plate for 5–10 minutes, until cooked to your taste.

To make the sauce, put the brandy and stock in a pan. Bring to the boil, then reduce the heat. Stir in the cream, horseradish and sugar and heat through. Serve with the steaks.

Serves 4

Thai red chicken with jasmine rice and Asian greens

1 tablespoon red curry paste
250 g (1 cup) coconut cream
3 makrut (kaffir) lime leaves
4 chicken breast fillets, tenderloin
  removed
400 g (2 cups) jasmine rice
250 ml (1 cup) chicken stock
1 tablespoon soy sauce
1 garlic clove, bruised
2 x 2 cm ($^3/_4$ x $^3/_4$ inch) piece fresh
  ginger, bruised
750 g (1 lb 10 oz) Chinese broccoli,
  washed and tied in a bunch
coriander (cilantro) sprigs

Mix together the curry paste, coconut cream and kaffir lime leaves, then add the chicken and turn it so that it is coated in the marinade. Cover the bowl and refrigerate it for at least 4 hours, or overnight.

Half an hour before you are ready to cook the chicken, wash the rice in a sieve until the water runs clear. Put the rice in a saucepan with 750 ml (3 cups) water and bring it to the boil for 1 minute. Cover the saucepan with a tightly fitting lid, reduce the heat to as low as possible and let it cook for 10 minutes. Without removing the lid, remove the pan from the heat and leave it for at least 10 minutes, or until you are ready to eat. Meanwhile, bring the chicken stock, soy sauce, garlic and gingor to tho boil in a small saucepan for 5 minutes, or until it is reduced by half. Strain the mixture, return the liquid to the saucepan and keep it warm.

Bring a large pot of salted water to the boil and add the Chinese broccoli, stalk-side down. Cook for 2–3 minutes or until it is just tender, then drain well and arrange it on a serving dish. Just before serving, pour the hot chicken stock mixture over the greens.

Preheat the flat grill plate to medium direct heat. Cook the chicken for 7–8 minutes on each side, or until it is cooked through. Transfer the chicken to a plate, cover it loosely with foil and leave it to rest. Fluff the rice with a fork and put it in a serving bowl. Garnish the chicken with coriander sprigs and serve it with the rice and Chinese broccoli.

Serves 4

Sumac-crusted lamb fillets with baba ganouj

2 tablespoons olive oil
750 g (1 lb 10 oz) small new potatoes
2–3 garlic cloves, crushed
60 ml (¼ cup) lemon juice
1 red capsicum (pepper), seeded and quartered lengthways
4 lamb backstraps (about 200 g/7 oz each)
1 tablespoon sumac (if unavailable, use ground cumin)
3 tablespoons finely chopped flat-leaf (Italian) parsley
250 g (9 oz) good-quality baba ganouj (eggplant (aubergine) dip)

Heat the oil in a saucepan big enough to hold the potatoes in one layer. Add the potatoes and garlic, and cook, turning frequently, for 3–5 minutes. When golden, add the lemon juice and reduce the heat to medium–low. Simmer, covered, for 15–20 minutes, or until tender (stir occasionally to prevent sticking). Remove from the heat and season well.

Meanwhile, lightly oil a barbecue chargrill plate and heat to very hot. Cook the capsicum skin-side down for 1–2 minutes, or until the skin starts to blister and turn black. Cook the other side for 1–2 minutes. Place in a plastic bag and set aside.

Coat the lamb with sumac. Cook on the chargrill plate for 4–5 minutes on each side, or until cooked to your liking. Remove from the heat, cover with foil and rest. Remove the skin from the capsicum and slice the quarters into thin strips.

Stir the parsley through the potatoes. Divide the baba ganouj among four plates. Cut the lamb into 1 cm (½ inch) slices on the diagonal and arrange on top of the baba ganouj with the capsicum strips. Serve with the potatoes and a green salad.

Serves 4

Veal steaks with caper butter

50 g (1³/₄ oz) butter, softened
2 tablespoons dry white wine
2 tablespoons capers, finely chopped
2 teaspoons finely grated lemon zest
8 small veal steaks, about 500 g
  (1 lb 2 oz)
mixed salad greens, to serve

Mix together the butter, white wine, capers, lemon zest and some salt and black pepper with a wooden spoon. Shape into a log, cover and refrigerate until required.

Cook the veal steaks on a hot, lightly oiled barbecue flat plate or grill for 2–3 minutes on each side. Remove, place on warm plates and top with slices of the caper butter. Serve immediately on a bed of salad greens.

Serves 4

Portuguese spatchcock

1 red onion, chopped
6 garlic cloves, chopped
3 teaspoons grated lemon zest
2 teaspoons chilli flakes
1½ teaspoons paprika
60 ml (¼ cup) oil
60 ml (¼ cup) red wine vinegar
4 x 500 g (1 lb 2 oz) spatchcocks
   (poussin)
10 g (⅓ cup) chopped flat-leaf
   (Italian) parsley
lemon halves

Put the onion, garlic, lemon zest, chilli flakes, paprika, oil and vinegar in a food processor and blend them to a smooth paste.

Cut each of the spatchcocks down the backbone with sharp kitchen scissors and press down on the breastbone to flatten it out. Score the flesh and brush it with the spice mixture, then put the spatchcocks in a non-metallic dish, cover and refrigerate overnight.

Preheat the chargrill plate to low–medium direct heat. Grill the spatchcocks for 10 minutes on each side, or until they are cooked through (test by piercing the thigh with a skewer — if the juices run clear, they are ready), then sprinkle with parsley and serve with the lemon halves.

Serves 4

Note: Try grilling the lemon halves for a bit of extra flavour.

Piri piri prawns

1 kg (2 lb 4 oz) large raw prawns
  (shrimp)
4 long red chillies, seeded
185 ml ($^3/_4$ cup) white wine vinegar
2 large garlic cloves, chopped
6–8 small red chillies, chopped
125 ml ($^1/_2$ cup) olive oil
150 g (5$^1/_2$ oz) mixed lettuce leaves

Remove the heads from the prawns and slice them down the back without cutting right through, leaving the tail intact. Open out each prawn and remove the dark vein, then store the prepared prawns in the refrigerator while you make the sauce.

To make the sauce, put the long chillies in a saucepan with the vinegar and simmer them over medium–high heat for 5 minutes, or until the chillies are soft. Let the mixture cool slightly, then put the chillies and 60 ml (¼ cup) of the vinegar in a food processor. Add the garlic and chopped small chillies, and blend until the mixture is smooth. While the motor is running, gradually add the oil and remaining vinegar to the food processor.

Put the prawns in the marinade, making sure they are well coated, then cover them and refrigerate for 30 minutes.

Take the prawns out of the marinade, bring the marinade to the boil and let it simmer for 5 minutes, or until it is slightly thickened and reduced. Take the prawns and the marinade out to the barbecue, and leave the saucepan with the marinade in it on the edge of the barbecue to keep warm.

Lightly oil the chargrill plate and heat it to high direct heat. Cook the prawns, basting them with the marinade, for 2–3 minutes on each side, or until they are cooked through. Arrange the lettuce on four plates, top it with the prawns and serve immediately with the chilli sauce.

Serves 4

Chargrilled vegetables with basil aïoli

Basil aïoli
1 garlic clove
15 g (¼ cup) torn basil leaves
1 egg yolk
125 ml (½ cup) olive oil
2 teaspoons lemon juice

2 large red capsicums (peppers),
   quartered, core and seeds removed
1 eggplant (aubergine), cut in 5 mm
   (¼ inch) thick rounds
1 orange sweet potato, peeled and
   cut on the diagonal into 5 mm
   (¼ inch) thick rounds
3 zucchini (courgettes), sliced
   lengthways into 5 mm (¼ inch)
   thick slices
2 red onions, cut into 1 cm (½ inch)
   thick rounds
80 ml (⅓ cup) olive oil
1 loaf Turkish bread, split and cut
   into 4 equal pieces

To make the basil aïoli, put the garlic, basil and egg yolk in a food processor and blend until smooth. With the motor running, gradually add the oil in a thin stream until the mixture thickens. Stir in the lemon juice and season to taste. Cover and refrigerate until you are ready to dish up.

Preheat a barbecue chargrill plate to medium direct heat. Put the capsicum, skin-side down, around the cool edge of the grill and cook it for 8–10 minutes or until the skin has softened and is blistering.

Meanwhile, brush the eggplant, sweet potato, zucchini and onion slices on both sides with olive oil and season them lightly. Cook the vegetables in batches on the middle of the chargrill for 5–8 minutes, or until they are cooked through but still firm. As the vegetable pieces cook, put them on a tray in a single layer to prevent them from steaming, then grill the Turkish bread on both sides until it is lightly marked and toasted.

Spread both cut sides of the bread with 1 tablespoon of basil aïoli and pile on some of the chargrilled vegetables. Top with the remaining toast and serve immediately.

Serves 4

Beef fajitas

800 g (1 lb 12 oz) rump steak
2 teaspoons ground cumin
1 teaspoon ground oregano
1 teaspoon paprika
2 tablespoons Worcestershire
sauce
1 tablespoon soy sauce
3 garlic cloves
60 ml (¼ cup) lime juice
1 large onion, thinly sliced
1 red capsicum (pepper), cut into
5 mm (¼ inch) strips
1 green capsicum (pepper),
cut into 5 mm (¼ inch) strips
1 tablespoon olive oil
8 flour tortillas
1 ripe avocado, diced
2 ripe Roma (plum) tomatoes,
diced
60 g (½ cup) grated Cheddar
cheese
90 g (⅓ cup) sour cream

Trim the steak of any fat and give it a good pounding with a meat mallet on both sides. Mix the cumin, oregano, paprika, Worcestershire sauce, soy sauce, garlic and lime juice in a shallow, non-metallic dish and add the beef. Turn until well coated in the marinade, then cover and refrigerate for at least 4 hours, or overnight.

Drain the steak, reserving the marinade, and pat it dry with paper towels. Simmer the marinade in a small saucepan over medium heat for 5 minutes, or until it is reduced by about half, and keep it warm.

Preheat a barbecue to high direct heat. Toss the onion and capsicum with the oil then spread them across the flat plate, turning every so often, for 10 minutes, or until cooked through and caramelized. While the vegetables are cooking, grill the steak on the chargrill plate for 3 minutes each side, or until cooked to your liking. Remove it from the heat and let it rest, covered, for 5 minutes. Thinly slice the steak and arrange it on a plate with the onion and capsicum strips and serve with the tortillas, avocado, tomato, cheese, sour cream and marinade sauce. Let everyone fill their own tortillas.

Serves 4–6

Crispy chicken wings

12 chicken wings
3 tablespoons soy sauce
3 tablespoons hoisin sauce
125 g (½ cup) tomato sauce
2 tablespoons honey
1 tablespoon soft brown sugar
1 tablespoon cider vinegar
2 garlic cloves, crushed
¼ teaspoon Chinese five-spice
   powder
2 teaspoons sesame oil

Tuck the chicken wing tips to the underside and place in a non-metallic bowl. Mix together all the remaining ingredients and pour over the wings, tossing to coat. Cover and leave in the fridge for at least 2 hours, turning occasionally. Drain, reserving the marinade.

Cook the wings on a hot, lightly oiled barbecue grill or flat plate for 5 minutes, or until cooked through, brushing with the reserved marinade several times.

Serves 6

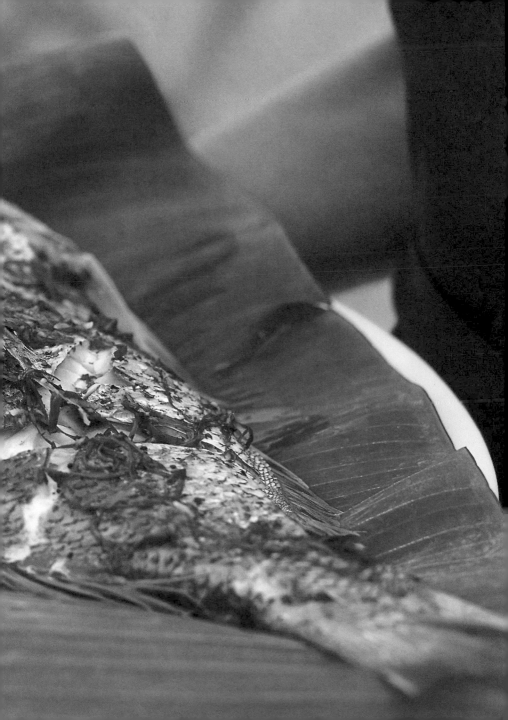

Snapper envelope with ginger and spring onions

Dressing
1 spring onion (scallion)
3 tablespoons coriander (cilantro)
    leaves
1 teaspoon finely grated fresh
    ginger
2 tablespoons lime juice
1 tablespoon fish sauce
½ teaspoon sesame oil

1 whole snapper (about 1.8–2 kg/
    4 lb–4 lb 8 oz)
sea salt
1 lime
4 spring onions (scallions)
30 g (1 cup) coriander (cilantro)
    leaves
1 tablespoon finely grated fresh
    ginger
canola oil spray

To make the dressing, finely slice the green part of the spring onion and the coriander leaves, and mix them together with the ginger, lime juice, fish sauce and sesame oil.

Check that the snapper has been thoroughly scaled, then wash it under cold running water and pat it dry with paper towels. In the thickest part of the flesh make diagonal cuts 1.5 cm (5/8 inch) apart in one direction, then in the other direction, so that the flesh is scored in a diamond pattern. Lightly season the fish with sea salt and freshly ground black pepper.

Peel the lime, removing all the pith, with a small, sharp knife and separate the lime sections by carefully cutting each piece away from the membrane. Slice the spring onions on the diagonal, mix them with tho coriander loaves, lime segments and ginger, and stuff the mixture into the cavity of the fish.

Lightly spray a double layer of foil with canola oil, making sure it is large enough to wrap around the fish and totally enclose it. Fold the foil around the fish and seal the edges tightly.

Preheat a kettle or covered barbecue to medium indirect heat. Put the fish in the middle of the barbecue and

cook it, covered, for 10 minutes. Use a large metal spatula to turn the fish so that it will brown evenly on both sides and cook it for another 8–10 minutes, or until it flakes when tested in the thickest part of the flesh.

When the fish is cooked, open the foil envelope and slide it onto a serving plate. Pour the cooking juices over the fish, drizzle the dressing over the top and serve straight away. It is delicious with steamed jasmine rice and a green salad.

Serves 4

Ginger-orange pork

6 pork butterfly steaks
250 ml (1 cup) ginger wine
150 g (½ cup) orange marmalade
2 tablespoons oil
1 tablespoon grated fresh ginger

Trim the pork steak of excess fat and sinew. Mix together the wine, marmalade, oil and ginger. Place the steaks in a shallow non-metallic dish and add the marinade. Store, covered with plastic wrap, in the fridge for at least 3 hours, turning occasionally. Drain, reserving the marinade.

Cook the pork on a hot, lightly oiled barbecue flat plate or grill for 5 minutes each side or until tender, turning once.

While the meat is cooking, place the reserved marinade in a small pan. Bring to the boil, reduce the heat and simmer for 5 minutes, or until the marinade has reduced and thickened slightly. Pour over the pork.

Serves 6

Hint: Steaks of uneven thickness may curl when cooked. Prevent this by leaving a layer of fat on the outside and making a few deep cuts in it prior to cooking. Remove before serving.

Lamb cutlets with mint gremolata

4 tablespoons mint leaves
1 tablespoon flat-leaf (Italian) parsley
2 garlic cloves
1½ tablespoons lemon zest (white pith removed), cut into thin strips
2 tablespoons extra virgin olive oil
8 French-trimmed lamb cutlets
2 carrots
2 zucchini (courgettes)
1 tablespoon lemon juice

To make the gremolata, finely chop the mint, parsley, garlic and lemon strips, then combine well.

Heat a chargrill pan or barbecue plate to very hot. Lightly brush with 1 tablespoon of the oil. Season the cutlets and cook over medium heat for 2 minutes on each side, or until cooked to your liking. Remove the cutlets and cover to keep warm.

Trim the ends from the carrots and zucchini and, using a vegetable peeler, peel the vegetables lengthways into ribbons. Heat the remaining oil in a large saucepan, add the vegetables and toss over medium heat for 3–5 minutes, or until sautéed but tender. Season lightly.

Divide the lamb cutlets among the serving plates, sprinkle the cutlets with the gremolata and drizzle with the lemon juice. Serve with the vegetable ribbons.

Serves 4

Bruschetta with mushrooms and mustard crème fraîche

5 small field mushrooms (about
  300 g/10½ oz), quartered
1 red onion, halved and thinly sliced
170 ml (²/₃ cup) olive oil
3 garlic cloves, crushed
1½ tablespoons chopped oregano
  leaves
60 g (¼ cup) crème fraîche
1 teaspoon Dijon mustard
1 loaf ciabatta bread
60 ml (¼ cup) olive oil, extra
1 large garlic clove, extra, peeled
  and halved
small oregano leaves
150 g (6 handfuls) mixed lettuce
  leaves
2 tablespoons extra virgin olive oil
1 tablespoon lemon juice

Put the mushrooms and onion in separate bowls and season each well. Whisk together the oil, garlic and oregano and pour two-thirds of the mixture over the mushrooms and the rest over the onion. Toss until well coated in the marinade, then cover and refrigerate for 30 minutes. Mix the crème fraîche and mustard together, then refrigerate it until needed.

Heat a barbecue to medium direct heat. Cut the bread into twelve 1 cm (½ inch) thick slices and brush both sides of each slice with the extra oil. Toast the bread on the chargrill plate for 1–2 minutes on each side or until golden and lightly charred, then rub one side of each slice with the cut side of the garlic clove. Cook the onion on the flat plate, tossing gently, for 2–3 minutes or until soft and golden. Cook the mushrooms on the flat plate for 2 minutes each side or until cooked through, then toss the onion and mushrooms together.

Arrange the mushrooms and onion on the garlic side of the bread slices and top with a teaspoon of mustard crème fraîche. Garnish with oregano leaves and season. Toss the lettuce leaves with the extra virgin olive oil and lemon juice, and serve with the bruschetta.

Serves 6

Miso-glazed salmon and eggplant salad with sesame dressing

5 tablespoons sesame seeds,
 lightly toasted
70 g (¼ cup) white miso
1 tablespoon sake
1 tablespoon mirin
1 tablespoon sugar
60 ml (¼ cup) dashi stock
1 large eggplant (aubergine),
 cut into 1 cm (½ inch) rounds
2 garlic cloves, crushed
60 ml (¼ cup) olive oil
2 teaspoons dark soy sauce
60 ml (¼ cup) dashi stock, extra
1 teaspoon sugar, extra
1 teaspoon grated fresh ginger
150 g (5½ oz) snowpea (mangetout)
 shoots
400 g (14 oz) daikon, julienned
4 salmon fillets, skin removed

To make the miso glaze, put the sesame seeds in a spice grinder or mortar and pestle and grind until they have a rough, flaky texture. Whisk the miso, sake, mirin, sugar and dashi stock together until smooth and stir in half of the crushed sesame seeds.

Put the eggplant rounds in a large bowl with the combined garlic and oil, season them well and toss until the rounds are well coated.

To make the dressing, whisk together the soy sauce, extra dashi and sugar, ginger and remaining crushed sesame seeds. Put the snowpea shoots and daikon in a large bowl, add the soy dressing and toss until well combined. Cover and refrigerate until needed.

Heat a barbecue to medium–high direct heat. Chargrill the eggplant for 3–4 minutes on each side, or until it has softened, then allow it to cool slightly and cut it into quarters. Brush both sides of each salmon fillet with the miso glaze and cook them on the flat plate for 2 minutes each side, or until they are almost cooked through, brushing with the glaze while they are cooking. Flake the fillets with a fork and toss them through the salad with the eggplant. Season and serve.

Serves 4

Lemon and thyme roasted chicken with zucchini

1 x 1.8 kg (4 lb) chicken
12 garlic cloves, unpeeled
10 sprigs lemon thyme
1 lemon, halved
1 tablespoon olive oil
8 small zucchini (courgettes),
    halved lengthways
2 tablespoons chopped flat-leaf
    (Italian) parsley
1 tablespoon plain (all-purpose)
    flour
250 ml (1 cup) chicken stock

Remove the giblets and any large fat deposits from inside the chicken, then pat it dry inside and out with paper towels. Season the cavity with salt and pepper and stuff it with the unpeeled garlic cloves and the sprigs of thyme. Rub the skin with the cut lemon, making sure that it is evenly coated all over, then brush it with 2 teaspoons of the oil and season with salt and black pepper. Tie the legs together.

Preheat a kettle or covered barbecue to medium indirect heat, with a drip tray underneath the grill. Position the chicken on the barbecue directly over the drip tray, close the hood and roast the chicken for 1 hour, or until the juices run clear when it is pierced with a skewer between the thigh and the body.

When the chicken has been cooking for about 40 minutes, toss the zucchini with the remaining olive oil and season it with salt and black pepper. Arrange the zucchini on the grill around the chicken, re-cover the kettle and cook the chicken and the zucchini for 20–25 minutes, or until the zucchini is tender, but not soggy. Put the zucchini in a serving dish and sprinkle it with the parsley. When the chicken is ready, remove it from the barbecue, cover it loosely with foil

and leave it to rest for 10 minutes. Remove the garlic from the chicken cavity but do not peel the cloves.

If you would like gravy to go with the chicken, pour the contents of the drip tray into a container and skim off as much fat as possible. Tip the remaining juices into a saucepan, add the flour and stir well to combine. Cook the gravy over medium heat for 3–4 minutes, or until it has thickened, then add the chicken stock and any juices that have been released from the chicken while it was resting. Bring the gravy to the boil, then reduce the heat and simmer it for 3–4 minutes. Season the gravy to taste, strain it into a jug and serve with the chicken, garlic and zucchini.

Serves 4

Thai beef salad

80 ml (⅓ cup) lime juice
2 tablespoons fish sauce
2 teaspoons grated palm sugar
   or soft brown sugar
1 garlic clove, crushed
1 tablespoon finely chopped
   coriander (cilantro) roots and stems
1 stem lemon grass (white part only),
   finely chopped
2 small red chillies, finely sliced
2 x 200 g (7 oz) beef eye fillet steaks
150 g (5½ oz) mixed salad leaves
½ red onion, cut into thin wedges
15 g (½ cup) coriander (cilantro)
   leaves
7 g (⅓ cup) torn mint leaves
250 g (9 oz) cherry tomatoes, halved
1 Lebanese (short) cucumber, halved
   lengthways and thinly sliced on the
   diagonal

Mix together the lime juice, fish
sauce, palm sugar, garlic, chopped
coriander, lemon grass and chilli until
the sugar has dissolved.

Preheat a barbecue chargrill plate to
medium–high direct heat and cook
the steaks for 4 minutes on each side,
or until medium. Let the steaks cool,
then slice thinly across the grain.

Put the salad leaves, onion, coriander
leaves, mint, tomatoes and cucumber
in a large bowl, add the beef and
dressing, toss them together and
serve immediately.

Serves 4

Barbecued chermoula prawns

1 kg (2 lb 4 oz) raw medium prawns
(shrimp)
3 teaspoons hot paprika
2 teaspoons ground cumin
30 g (1 cup) flat-leaf (Italian) parsley
15 g (1/2 cup) coriander (cilantro)
leaves
100 ml (3 fl oz) lemon juice
145 ml (5 fl oz) olive oil
280 g (1 1/2 cups) couscous
1 tablespoon grated lemon zest
lemon wedges, to serve

Peel the prawns, leaving the tails intact, and discard the heads. Gently pull out the dark vein from the backs, starting at the head end. Place the prawns in a large bowl. Dry-fry the paprika and cumin in a frying pan for about 1 minute, or until fragrant. Remove from the heat.

Blend or process the spices, parsley, coriander, lemon juice and 125 ml (1/2 cup) of the oil until finely chopped. Add a little salt and pepper. Pour over the prawns and mix well, then cover with plastic wrap and refrigerate for 10 minutes. Heat a chargrill pan or barbecue plate to hot.

Meanwhile, to cook the couscous, bring 250 ml (1 cup) water to the boil in a saucepan, and stir in the couscous, lemon zest, the remaining oil and 1/4 teaspoon salt. Remove from the heat, cover and leave for 5 minutes. Fluff the couscous with a fork, adding a little extra olive oil if needed.

Cook the prawns on the chargrill plate for about 3–4 minutes, or until cooked through, turning and brushing with extra marinade while cooking (take care not to overcook). Serve the prawns on a bed of couscous, with a wedge of lemon.

Serves 4

Hoisin lamb with charred spring onion

800 g (1 lb 12 oz) lamb loin
60 ml (¼ cup) hoisin sauce
2 tablespoons soy sauce
2 garlic cloves, bruised
1 tablespoon grated fresh ginger
2 teaspoons olive oil
16 spring onions (scallions), trimmed
  to 18 cm (7 inches) long
40 g (¼ cup) chopped toasted
  peanuts

Trim the lamb of any excess fat and sinew. Combine the hoisin sauce, soy sauce, garlic, ginger and 1 teaspoon of the oil in a shallow dish, add the lamb and turn it so that it is well coated in the marinade. Cover the dish and refrigerate for 4 hours or overnight.

Toss the trimmed spring onions with the remaining oil and season them well. Remove the lamb from the marinade, season the meat and pour the marinade into a small saucepan. Simmer the marinade for 5 minutes, or until it is slightly reduced. Preheat a chargrill plate to medium direct heat. Cook the lamb for 5–6 minutes on each side, or until it is cooked to your liking, brushing it frequently with the reduced marinade, then let it rest, covered, for 3 minutes. Grill the spring onions for 1–2 minutes, or until they are tender, but still firm.

Cut the lamb across the grain into 2 cm (¾ inch) thick slices, and arrange it on a serving plate. Drizzle any juices that have been released during resting over the lamb and sprinkle it with the toasted peanuts. Serve with the spring onions. This is delicious with Asian rice salad (see page 317).

Serves 4

Spiced duck breast with peach and chilli salad

6 ripe peaches
1 lime plus 1 tablespoon lime juice, extra
1 tablespoon extra virgin olive oil
1 small red chilli, seeded and finely sliced
2 tablespoons chopped mint leaves
4 duck breasts
2 teaspoons ground coriander
lime wedges

Dip the peaches into a saucepan of boiling water for 5 seconds then plunge them into iced water. Remove the skins, which should slip off easily. Cut each peach in half, remove the stone, then cut each half into eight wedges. Peel the lime, removing all the pith, and separate the lime sections by carefully cutting each piece away from the membrane. Toss the peach slices with the lime segments, extra lime juice, olive oil, chilli and mint, and season with a little pepper.

Trim the duck breasts of fat and sinew, and sprinkle each breast with the ground coriander.

Preheat a barbecue flat plate to medium direct heat and cook the duck on the flat plate for 4 minutes or until the skin is golden, then turn it and cook for another 4 minutes. Turn the breasts over again and cook them for 1 minute longer to make the skin crispy, then leave to rest in a warm place for 10 minutes.

Slice each breast into four pieces on the diagonal and serve them with the peach salad and lime wedges.

Serves 4

Bourbon-glazed beef ribs with sweet potato

Marinade
¼ teaspoon chilli powder
½ teaspoon chilli flakes
½ teaspoon celery salt
⅛ teaspoon cayenne pepper
500 ml (2 cups) cider vinegar
60 ml (¼ cup) lemon juice
6 garlic cloves, crushed
1 tablespoon paprika
1 teaspoon garlic powder
1 teaspoon onion powder
125 ml (½ cup) Worcestershire sauce

3 kg (6 lb 8 oz) beef loin ribs

Sweet potatoes
60 g (2¼ oz) butter, at room
    temperature
1 tablespoon maple syrup
1 tablespoon chopped pecan nuts
½ teaspoon garlic salt
4 x 200 g (7 oz) sweet potatoes

Barbecue sauce
500 ml (2 cups) tomato sauce
55 g (¼ cup) soft brown sugar
80 ml (⅓ cup) bourbon
60 g (¼ cup) Dijon mustard
1 tablespoon Tabasco sauce
2 teaspoons paprika
1 teaspoon garlic powder
1 teaspoon onion powder
1½ tablespoons Worcestershire sauce

Put the marinade ingredients in a bowl with ¼ teaspoon pepper and ¼ teaspoon salt, mix together well and rub the marinade all over the ribs. Put the ribs in a non-metallic bowl, cover them and refrigerate overnight.

Mash together the butter, maple syrup, pecans, garlic salt and some black pepper, and cover until you are ready to dish up.

Put the barbecue sauce ingredients in a saucepan and stir together. Simmer over low heat for 15 minutes, or until the mixture has thickened, stirring constantly. Be careful while stirring the sauce as it might splatter a bit.

Preheat a kettle or covered barbecue to very low indirect heat. Remove the ribs from the marinade and baste them all over with the barbecue sauce. Cook them on the flat plate for 3 hours, or until they are very tender, turning and basting them every 30 minutes.

Arrange the whole sweet potatoes on a lightly greased baking tray and add them to the barbecue 45 minutes before the ribs have finished cooking.

Remove the ribs and sweet potatoes from the barbecue, slice each sweet potato down the middle and top each

with some of the flavoured butter. Cut between the ribs to separate them and serve the ribs with the sweet potatoes.

Serves 4–6

Notes: Beef loin ribs are also known as beef shortribs.
Make sure the barbecue temperature remains low and constant. If the heat is too high, the ribs will burn before they become tender.

Stuffed eggplant

2 eggplants (aubergines)
2 tablespoons olive oil
1 onion, chopped
2 garlic cloves, crushed
4 tomatoes, roughly chopped
2 teaspoons tomato paste
    (tomato purée)
2 tablespoons chopped dill
2 tablespoons chopped flat-leaf
    (Italian) parsley
2 tablespoons currants
2 tablespoons pine nuts
1 tablespoon red wine vinegar
150 g (1½ cups) finely grated
    kefalotyri cheese

Cut each eggplant in half lengthways and use a sharp knife to cut out the flesh, leaving a 5 mm (¼ inch) thick shell. Finely dice the flesh, toss it with 2 teaspoons of salt and drain it in a colander over a bowl for 30 minutes. Squeeze out any excess moisture from the eggplant, rinse it under cold water and drain well on paper towels.

Heat 1 tablespoon oil in a frying pan over high heat. Add the diced eggplant and cook it, stirring frequently, for 5 minutes, or until browned. Transfer to a large bowl. Heat the remaining olive oil in the frying pan over medium heat, cook the onion and garlic for 2 minutes, then add the tomato, tomato paste, dill, parsley, currants, pine nuts and vinegar. Stir it all together and cook for 8–10 minutes, stirring occasionally. Add the tomato mixture to the eggplant with 100 g (1 cup) of the kefalotyri, season with black pepper and mix it together well.

Spoon the vegetable mixture into the eggplant shells and sprinkle with the remaining cheese. Preheat a kettle or covered barbecue to medium indirect heat and put the eggplants in the middle of the barbecue. Cover and cook for 30 minutes, or until cooked through. Serve with a green salad.

Serves 4

Tuna steaks with salsa and garlic mash

Garlic mash
1 kg (2 lb 4 oz) floury (starchy)
    potatoes, cut into chunks
6–8 garlic cloves, peeled
80 ml (⅓ cup) milk
60 ml (¼ cup) olive oil

Salsa
1 tablespoon olive oil
2 French shallots, finely chopped
200 g (7 oz) green olives, pitted
    and quartered lengthways
35 g (¼ cup) currants, soaked in
    warm water for 10 minutes
1 tablespoon baby capers, rinsed
    and squeezed dry
1 tablespoon sherry vinegar
2 tablespoons shredded mint
    leaves

4 tuna steaks (about 150 g/5½ oz
    each)
olive oil, for brushing
sea salt

Boil the potato chunks and garlic for 10–15 minutes, or until tender. Drain them, then return the pan to the heat, shaking it to evaporate any excess water. Remove the pan from the heat and mash the potato and garlic until smooth, then stir in the milk and olive oil, and season with salt and freshly ground black pepper.

To make the salsa, heat the oil in a frying pan over medium heat. Cook the shallots for 2–4 minutes, or until they are softened, but not browned, then add the olives, drained currants and capers. Cook for 2 minutes, stirring continuously, then add the vinegar and cook for 2 minutes, or until the liquid is reduced by about half. Remove the pan from the heat and keep the salsa warm until you're ready to dish up.

Preheat a barbecue chargrill plate to medium–high direct heat. Brush the tuna steaks with olive oil, season them well with sea salt and freshly ground black pepper, and grill for 2–3 minutes each side for medium–rare, or until they are cooked to your liking. Stir the mint into the salsa and serve it immediately with the garlic mash and tuna.

Serves 4

Malaysian barbecued seafood

1 onion, grated
4 garlic cloves, chopped
5 cm (2 inch) piece of fresh ginger, grated
3 stems lemon grass (white part only), chopped
2 teaspoons ground or grated fresh turmeric
1 teaspoon shrimp paste
80 ml (1/3 cup) vegetable oil
1/4 teaspoon salt
4 medium calamari tubes
2 thick white boneless fish fillets
8 raw king prawns (shrimp)
banana leaves, for serving
2 limes, cut into wedges
strips of lime zest, to garnish
mint leaves, to garnish

Combine the onion, garlic, ginger, lemon grass, turmeric, shrimp paste, oil and salt in a small food processor. Process in short bursts until the mixture forms a paste.

Cut the calamari in half lengthways and lay it on the bench with the soft inside facing up. Score a very fine honeycomb pattern into the soft side, taking care not to cut all the way through, and then cut into large pieces. Wash all the seafood under cold running water and pat dry with paper towels. Brush lightly with the spice paste, then place on a tray, cover and refrigerate for 15 minutes.

Lightly oil a chargrill plate and heat. When the plate is hot, arrange the fish fillets and prawns on the plate. Cook, turning once only, for about 3 minutes each side or until the fish flesh is just firm and the prawns turn bright pink to orange. Add the calamari pieces and cook for about 2 minutes or until the flesh turns white and rolls up. Take care not to overcook the seafood.

Arrange the seafood on a platter lined with the banana leaves, add the lime wedges and serve immediately, garnished with strips of lime zest and some fresh mint.

Serves 4

Crispy-skinned salmon salad niçoise

400 g (14 oz) kipfler potatoes,
  washed
1 tablespoon olive oil
sea salt
12 quail eggs
300 g (10½ oz) small green beans
2 teaspoons olive oil, extra
3 x 200 g (7 oz) salmon fillets
2 large ripe tomatoes, cut into
  8 wedges
150 g (5½ oz) small black olives
80 ml (⅓ cup) extra virgin olive oil
1½ tablespoons white wine vinegar
1 tablespoon lemon juice
2 garlic cloves, crushed

Boil or steam the potatoes for 10 minutes or until they are almost cooked through. Drain and cut them into 2 cm (³/₄ inch) slices on the diagonal, then toss them with the olive oil until they are coated. Season to taste with sea salt.

Put the eggs in a saucepan of cold water and bring them to the boil for 2 minutes. Cool the eggs under running water, then peel and halve them. Bring the water back to the boil and cook the beans for 2 minutes or until they are just tender, then drain them, plunge them into cold water and drain again.

Heat the barbecue to medium–high direct heat. Cook the potato slices on the chargrill plate for 2 minutes on each side, or until they are golden and cooked through. Brush the salmon fillets with the extra oil and cook them, skin-side down, on the flat plate for 2–3 minutes, then turn and cook them for another 2–3 minutes, or until they are almost cooked through. The salmon should remain slightly rare in the middle. Break the filletsinto chunks with a fork, removing any bones as you go.

Put the potato in a large bowl with the beans, tomato and olives. Whisk together the oil, vinegar, lemon juice and garlic, and add the dressing to the bowl. Season with sea salt and freshly ground black pepper, and gently toss the salad until everything is well combined. Pile some of the potato mixture on four serving plates, top with the salmon and eggs, and serve immediately.

Serves 4

Pork loin with apple glaze and wedges

1 teaspoon aniseed
135 g (½ cup) apple sauce
2 tablespoons soft brown sugar
1.5 kg (3 lb 5 oz) boned pork loin
  with the skin on
2 teaspoons oil
4 large potatoes, each cut into
  8 wedges
2 tablespoons olive oil
2 teaspoons garlic salt

Dry-fry the aniseed over medium heat for 30 seconds, or until it becomes fragrant. Add the apple sauce and brown sugar, reduce the heat to low and cook, stirring, for 1 minute.

Use a sharp knife to remove the skin from the pork loin. Score the skin in a diamond pattern and rub the oil and 1 tablespoon salt over the skin, working into the cuts. Put the potato wedges in a bowl with the olive oil and garlic salt, season with black pepper and toss until well coated.

Preheat a kettle or covered barbecue to medium indirect heat. Tie the pork loin with string to help keep its shape, then put the pork and the skin in the barbecue and arrange the wedges around them. After 30 minutes, baste the pork with the apple glaze, and repeat every 10 minutes for another 30 minutes (for 1 hour cooking time in all). Turn the skin and the wedges as you go so that they cook evenly.

When the pork is ready, remove it from the barbecue and leave to rest, covered, for 10 minutes before carving. Cut the crackling with a sharp knife, arrange it on a platter with the pork and serve with the wedges. Delicious with dill coleslaw (see page 330).

Serves 6–8

Lamb souvlaki roll

500 g (1 lb 2 oz) lamb backstrap
  or loin fillet
100 ml (3½ fl oz) olive oil
3 tablespoons dry white wine
1 tablespoon chopped oregano
3 tablespoons roughly chopped basil
3 garlic cloves, crushed
2 bay leaves, crushed
2½ tablespoons lemon juice
1 large loaf Turkish bread
250 g (1 cup) baba ganouj (eggplant
  (aubergine) dip)
1 tablespoon roughly chopped
  flat-leaf (Italian) parsley

Place the lamb fillet in a shallow non-metallic dish. Mix together the oil, wine, oregano, basil, garlic, bay leaves and 2 tablespoons of the lemon juice and pour over the lamb, turning to coat well. Cover with plastic wrap and marinate for 4 hours.

Remove the lamb fillet from the marinade and cook on a hot, lightly oiled barbecue grill or flat plate for 6–8 minutes, or until seared but still pink in the centre. Remove from the heat and rest for 10 minutes, then cut into slices.

Split the Turkish bread lengthways and spread the bottom thickly with baba ganouj. Top with the lamb slices, sprinkle with the parsley and remaining lemon juice, then season with salt and pepper. Replace the top of the loaf, then cut into quarters to serve.

Serves 4

Spicy crab with Singapore-style pepper sauce

2 kg (4 lb 8 oz) blue crabs
150 g (5½ oz) butter
2 tablespoons finely chopped garlic
1 tablespoon finely chopped fresh
  ginger
1 small red chilli, seeded and finely
  chopped
3 tablespoons ground black pepper
2 tablespoons dark soy sauce
2 tablespoons oyster sauce
1 tablespoon palm sugar or soft
  brown sugar
1 spring onion (scallion), green part
  only, sliced thinly on the diagonal

Pull back the apron and remove the top shell from each crab (it should come off in one piece). Remove the intestine and the grey feathery gills, then use a sharp knife to cut the crab in half lengthways, leaving the legs attached. Crack the thick part of the legs with the back of a heavy knife or crab crackers to make it easier to extract the meat.

Heat a barbecue flat plate or chargrill plate to medium–high direct heat. Cook the crabs for 5–8 minutes on each side, or until they turn orange and are cooked through. Heat a wok over medium heat (you'll need to do this on the stovetop if you don't have a wok burner on your barbecue), and stir-fry the butter, garlic, ginger, chilli and pepper for 30 seconds or until fragrant. Add the combined soy and oyster sauces and sugar and simmer for 1 minute or until glossy.

Toss the cooked crab in the sauce until it is completely coated, then arrange it on a serving dish, sprinkle with the spring onion and serve with steamed rice and a green salad. This dish is very rich and very messy to eat — make sure there are plenty of paper towels or napkins on hand to clear up spills.

Serves 4–6

Lime and coriander chargrilled chicken

3 teaspoons finely grated fresh
 ginger
25 g (½ cup) chopped coriander
 (cilantro) leaves
1½ teaspoons grated lime zest
80 ml (⅓ cup) lime juice
4 skinless chicken breast fillets
 (about 750 g/1lb 10 oz), trimmed
250 g (1¼ cups) jasmine rice
2 tablespoons oil
3 zucchini (courgettes), cut into
 wedges
4 large flat mushrooms, stalks
 trimmed

Combine the ginger, coriander, lime zest and 2 tablespoons of the lime juice. Spread 2 teaspoons of the herb mixture over each fillet and season well. Marinate for 1 hour. Combine the remaining herb mixture with the remaining lime juice in a screwtop jar. Set aside until needed.

Bring a large saucepan of water to the boil. Add the rice and cook for 12 minutes, stirring occasionally. Drain well.

Meanwhile, heat a barbecue plate to medium and lightly brush with oil. Brush the zucchini and mushrooms with the remaining oil. Place the chicken on the chargrill plate and cook on each side for 4–5 minutes, or until cooked through. Add the vegetables during the last 5 minutes of cooking, and turn frequently until browned on the outside and just softened. Cover with foil until ready to serve.

Divide the rice among four serving bowls. Cut the chicken fillets into long thick strips, then arrange on top of the rice. Shake the dressing well and drizzle over the chicken and serve with the chargrilled vegetables.

Serves 4

Lamb stuffed with olives, feta and oregano

85 g (½ cup) Kalamata olives,
    pitted
3 garlic cloves, crushed
100 ml (3½ fl oz) olive oil
800 g (1 lb 12 oz) lamb sirloin,
    trimmed (see Note)
90 g (3¼ oz) feta cheese, crumbled
2 tablespoons oregano leaves,
    finely shredded
80 ml (⅓ cup) lemon juice

Put the Kalamata olives in a food processor or blender with the garlic and 2 tablespoons of olive oil, and blend until it is smooth. Season to taste with ground black pepper.

Prepare the sirloin by cutting horizontally most of the way through the piece, starting at one end, leaving a small join at the other end. Open out the lamb so you have a piece half as thick and twice as long as you started with.

Spread the olive and garlic paste in a thin, even layer over the cut surface of the lamb, then crumble the feta over the top and scatter with the chopped oregano. Roll the lamb tightly, starting with one of the long cut edges, and tie the whole length with cooking twine, so that the filling is contained and secure.

Put the lamb into a dish large enough to hold it lying flat and drizzle it with the lemon juice and remaining olive oil, turning to make sure that all of the lamb is well coated. Cover the dish and refrigerate it for 3 hours.

Prepare a chargrill plate to medium–high direct heat. Season the lamb and grill it, turning to brown each side, for 10 minutes, or until it is cooked to your liking. Remove it

from the barbecue and let it rest, covered, for 5 minutes. Use a very sharp knife to cut the roll into 5 cm (2 inch) pieces on the diagonal and serve it immediately with a mixed green salad.

Serves 4

Note: Use the thick end of the sirloin for this recipe.

Chilli pork ribs

1 kg (2 lb 4 oz) pork spareribs
125 g (4½ oz) tin puréed tomatoes
2 tablespoons honey
2 tablespoons chilli sauce
2 tablespoons hoisin sauce
2 tablespoons lime juice
2 garlic cloves, crushed
1 tablespoon oil

Cut each rib into thirds, then lay them in a single layer in a shallow non-metallic dish.

Mix together all the other ingredients except the oil and pour over the meat, turning to coat well. Cover with plastic wrap and refrigerate overnight, turning occasionally.

Drain the ribs, reserving the marinade, and cook them over medium heat on a lightly oiled barbecue grill or flat plate. Baste often with the marinade and cook for 15–20 minutes, or until the ribs are tender and well browned, turning occasionally. Season to taste and serve immediately.

Serves 4–6

Grilled haloumi salad

1½ tablespoons lemon juice
2 tablespoons finely chopped mint
  leaves
125 ml (½ cup) olive oil
2 garlic cloves
8 slices ciabatta bread
300 g (10½ oz) haloumi cheese,
  cut into 5 mm (½ inch) slices
3 ripe tomatoes
150 g (5½ oz) rocket (arugula) leaves
2 tablespoons pine nuts, toasted

Whisk the lemon juice, mint, 60 ml (¼ cup) of olive oil and 1 clove of crushed garlic together, and season with salt and pepper.

Brush both sides of each slice of bread with 1 tablespoon of olive oil and season well. Brush the haloumi with 1 tablespoon of olive oil. Cut the tomatoes into 1 cm (½ inch) rounds, brush with 1 tablespoon olive oil and season well.

Preheat a barbecue to medium direct heat and chargrill the bread for 1 minute on each side, or until it is golden and marked. Rub each piece on both sides with the remaining clove of garlic. Wrap the toast in foil and keep it warm on the side of the barbecue. Chargrill the haloumi and tomato for 3–5 minutes on each side, or until they are browned, then drizzle with 1 tablespoon of the mint and lemon dressing.

Put the rocket and pine nuts in a large bowl, add the remaining dressing and toss gently until the salad is coated with the dressing. Pile some onto a piece of the garlic toast, arrange some grilled haloumi and tomato across the top and serve it warm.

Serves 4

Barbecued sardines

8 large fresh sardines
8 sprigs lemon thyme
3 tablespoons extra virgin olive oil
2 garlic cloves, crushed
1 teaspoon finely grated lemon zest
2 tablespoons lemon juice
1 teaspoon ground cumin
lemon wedges, for serving

Carefully slit the sardines from head to tail and remove the gut. Rinse, then pat dry inside and out with paper towels. Place a sprig of lemon thyme in each fish cavity and arrange the fish in a shallow non-metallic dish.

Combine the olive oil, garlic, lemon zest, lemon juice and cumin and pour over the fish. Cover and refrigerate for 2 hours.

Cook the sardines on a hot, lightly oiled barbecue flat plate, basting frequently with the marinade, for about 2–3 minutes each side or until the flesh flakes easily when tested with a fork. Alternatively, barbecue in a sardine cooking rack until tender. Serve hot with lemon wedges.

Serves 4

Roast lamb

2.5 kg (5 lb 8 oz) leg of lamb
6 garlic cloves, peeled
2 tablespoons rosemary leaves
1 tablespoon olive oil

Make 12 small incisions in the fleshy parts of the lamb. Cut the garlic cloves in half lengthways, and push them into the incisions with the rosemary leaves. Rub the lamb with the oil and season it liberally with salt and pepper. Preheat a kettle or covered barbecue to medium indirect heat, put the lamb in the middle of the barbecue, replace the lid, and let it roast for 1 hour 30 minutes.

When the lamb is ready, remove it from the barbecue and let it rest, covered, for 10 minutes before carving and serving it with any juices that have been released while it rested. This dish is sensational with ratatouille (see page 353).

Serves 6

Stuffed pork chops with chargrilled spring onions

2 tablespoons dry sherry

4 dried dessert figs

1 tablespoon butter

60 ml (¼ cup) olive oil

1 small onion, finely diced

2 garlic cloves, crushed

1 large Granny Smith apple, peeled,
cored and grated

2 tablespoons slivered almonds,
lightly toasted

1 tablespoon finely chopped sage
leaves

6 large pork loin chops (250 g/9 oz
each) on the bone

16 large bulb spring onions
(scallions), green parts removed,
halved

Bring the sherry and 1 tablespoon of water to the boil in a small saucepan. Soak the figs in the hot sherry mixture for about 20 minutes, then slice them finely and keep the soaking liquid to use later.

Heat the butter and 1 tablespoon of olive oil in a frying pan, add the onion and garlic, and cook over low heat for 5 minutes or until they are softened. Add the grated apple, figs and sherry liquid, and simmer for a further 5 minutes, or until the apple has softened and most of the liquid has evaporated. Remove the pan from the heat and stir in the almonds and sage, then season well and allow the mixture to cool.

Trim the pork chops of any excess fat and make an incision into the middle of the chop from the side. Be careful — you only want to make a pocket in the flesh and not cut right through. Fill the pocket with the apple and fig stuffing, pushing it well into the cavity so that none is spilling out — you should fit about $1\frac{1}{2}$ tablespoons of filling in each chop. Brush the chops all over with 1 tablespoon of the olive oil, and season with salt and freshly ground black pepper. Toss the spring onion with the remaining oil, and season it well.

Heat a barbecue chargrill plate to medium direct heat. Cook the chops for 8 minutes on each side, or until the outside is slightly charred and the meat is cooked through. While the chops are cooking, add the spring onions to the chargrill plate and cook them for 10 minutes, or until they are softened. Serve the chops and spring onions as soon as they come off the barbecue.

Serves 6

King prawns with dill mayonnaise

Marinade
125 ml (½ cup) olive oil
80 ml (⅓ cup) lemon juice
2 tablespoons wholegrain mustard
2 tablespoons honey
2 tablespoons chopped dill

16–20 raw king prawns (shrimp)

Dill mayonnaise
185 g (¾ cup) mayonnaise
2 tablespoons chopped dill
1½ tablespoons lemon juice
1 gherkin, finely chopped
1 teaspoon chopped capers
1 garlic clove, crushed

To make the marinade, combine the olive oil, lemon juice, mustard, honey and dill, pour over the unpeeled prawns and coat well. Cover and refrigerate for at least 2 hours, turning occasionally.

To make the dill mayonnaise, whisk together the mayonnaise, dill, lemon juice, gherkin, capers and garlic. Cover and refrigerate.

Cook the drained prawns on a hot, lightly oiled barbecue grill or flat plate in batches for 4 minutes, turning frequently until pink and cooked through. Serve with the mayonnaise.

Serves 4

Beef with blue cheese butter

100 g (3½ oz) butter, softened
2 garlic cloves, crushed
100 g (3½ oz) Blue Castello cheese
2 teaspoons finely shredded sage
  leaves
1 kg (2 lb 4 oz) beef eye fillet (thick
  end), trimmed
1 tablespoon olive oil

To make the blue cheese butter, mash together the softened butter, garlic, cheese and sage until they are well combined. Form the mixture into a log and wrap it in baking paper, twisting the ends to seal them. Refrigerate the butter until firm, then cut it into 5 mm (¼ inch) slices and leave it at room temperature until needed.

Cut the beef into four thick, equal pieces and tie a piece of string around the edge of each so it will keep its shape during cooking. Brush both sides of each steak with the oil and season with freshly ground pepper. Heat a barbecue to medium–high direct heat and cook the beef on the chargrill plate for 6–7 minutes each side for medium, or to your liking.

Put two slices of blue cheese butter on top of each steak as soon as you remove it from the barbecue and remove the string. This is delicious served with pear and walnut salad (see page 296).

Serves 4

Note: Any leftover butter can be wrapped in baking paper and foil, and frozen for up to 2 months. It is also delicious with chicken and pork.

Chicken Caesar salad

Caesar dressing
1 egg yolk
1 garlic clove, crushed
3 anchovy fillets
1 teaspoon Dijon mustard
125 ml (½ cup) oil
1 tablespoon lemon juice
½ teaspoon Worcestershire
  sauce
15 g (½ oz) grated Parmesan
  cheese

4 chicken thigh fillets, trimmed
  of fat and sinew
80 ml (⅓ cup) olive oil
12 x 1 cm (½ inch) thick slices
  baguette
1 garlic clove, halved
4 rashers bacon
2 baby cos (romaine) lettuces,
  well washed and drained
extra anchovies, optional

Put the egg yolk, garlic, anchovies and mustard in a food processor and blend them together. With the motor running, gradually add the oil in a thin stream and process until the mixture becomes thick. Stir in the lemon juice, Worcestershire sauce and Parmesan, and season with salt and pepper.
Put the chicken thighs in a bowl with 1 tablespoon of olive oil, season to taste and turn to coat well with the oil.

Preheat a barbecue chargrill plate to medium–high direct heat. Brush the baguette slices with the remaining olive oil, and toast on the chargrill plate for 1 minute each side, or until they are crisp and marked. Rub both sides of each piece of toast with the cut clove of garlic and keep warm.

Grill the chicken on the chargrill plate for 5 minutes on each side, or until cooked through. Leave to rest for 1 minute then cut into 1 cm (½ inch) strips. Cook the bacon for 3 minutes each side or until crispy, then break it into 2 cm (¾ inch) pieces.

Tear the cos leaves into bite-sized pieces and toss them in a large bowl with the dressing, bacon and chicken. Serve with the garlic croutons and let people add extra anchovies to taste.

Serves 4–6

Lamb fillets wrapped in vine leaves with avgolemono sauce

12 lamb fillets (approximately 700 g/
   1 lb 9 oz)
2 teaspoons lemon juice
1½ teaspoons ground cumin
2 tablespoons olive oil
1 kg (2 lb 4 oz) waxy potatoes
   (e.g. pink fir apple, kipfler)
12 large vine leaves preserved in
   brine

Avgolemono sauce
2 eggs
1 egg yolk
60 ml (¼ cup) lemon juice
100 ml (3½ fl oz) chicken
   stock

Trim the fillets and put them in a bowl with the lemon juice, cumin and 1 tablespoon of the olive oil, then turn the fillets so they are coated. Cover the bowl and leave the lamb to marinate for 1 hour. Steam or boil the potatoes for 10–15 minutes or until they are just tender. When they are cool enough to handle, peel them and slice each one in half lengthways. Toss the potato halves gently in the remaining olive oil, and season with salt and pepper.

Rinse the vine leaves under warm water, pat them dry with paper towels and remove any woody stems. Lay the leaf flat with the vein side facing up, remove the lamb from the marinade, season it well with salt and pepper, and put a lamb fillet on the bottom of each vine leaf. Roll up the leaf so that it is wrapped around the lamb with the join sitting underneath.

To make the avgolemono sauce, whisk the whole eggs, egg yolk and lemon juice together, then bring the chicken stock to the boil and add 1 tablespoon of the hot stock to the egg mixture. Mix them together, then slowly add the egg mixture to the stock, stirring continuously. Cook the sauce over low heat, stirring it constantly with a wooden spoon for 4–5 minutes, or until it thickens

enough to hold a line drawn across the back of the spoon. Take care not to let the sauce boil, or the mixture will curdle beyond redemption.

Preheat a barbecue to medium direct heat. Cook the potatoes on the chargrill plate for 6–7 minutes, or until they are golden and crisp and the lamb fillets for 1–2 minutes on each side for medium–rare, or until they are done to your liking.

Slice the lamb fillets in half on the diagonal and serve them with the sauce and grilled potatoes.

Serves 4

Scallops with sesame bok choy

24 large scallops with corals
2 tablespoons light soy sauce
1 tablespoon fish sauce
1 tablespoon honey
1 tablespoon kecap manis
grated zest and juice of 1 lime
2 teaspoons grated fresh ginger
lime wedges, to serve

Sesame bok choy
1 tablespoon sesame oil
1 tablespoon sesame seeds
1 garlic clove, crushed
8 baby bok choy (pak choi),
  halved lengthways

Rinse the scallops, remove the dark vein and dry with paper towels. Mix the soy and fish sauce, honey, kecap manis, lime rind and juice and ginger. Pour over the scallops, cover and refrigerate for 15 minutes. Drain, reserving the marinade.

To make the sesame bok choy, pour the oil onto a hot barbecue flat plate and add the sesame seeds and garlic. Cook, stirring, for 1 minute, or until the seeds are golden. Arrange the bok choy in a single layer on the hot plate and pour over the reserved marinade. Cook for 3–4 minutes, turning once, until tender. Remove and keep warm.

Wipe clean the flat plate, brush with oil and reheat. Add the scallops and cook, turning, for about 2 minutes, or until they become opaque. Serve on top of the bok choy, with the lime wedges.

Serves 4

Chilli bean tortilla wraps

Chilli beans
2 tablespoons olive oil
2 garlic cloves, crushed
1 onion, finely chopped
1 green capsicum (pepper),
   seeded, cored and chopped
2 small red chillies, seeded and
   finely chopped
½ teaspoon cayenne pepper
1 teaspoon paprika
1 teaspoon ground cumin
¼ teaspoon sugar
440 g (15½ oz) tin crushed
   tomatoes
440 g (15½ oz) tin red kidney
   beans, drained and rinsed
1 tablespoon tomato paste
   (tomato purée)

12 x 20 cm (8 inch) soft flour
   tortillas
225 g (8 oz) Cheddar cheese,
   coarsely grated
250 g (1 cup) sour cream
coriander (cilantro) sprigs,
   to garnish
1 lime, cut into 8 wedges

To make the chilli beans, heat the oil in a saucepan over low heat and cook the garlic, onion and capsicum, stirring frequently, for 8–10 minutes, or until the onion and capsicum have softened. Add the chilli, cayenne pepper, paprika, cumin, sugar, tomato, beans, tomato paste and 125 ml (½ cup) water. Bring the mixture to the boil, then reduce the heat and simmer for 15–20 minutes, or until it is thickened and reduced. Season to taste.

To assemble the wraps, put some of the chilli beans along the middle of each tortilla, sprinkle it with 2 tablespoons of the cheese and roll it up. Put three rolls, seam-side down, on a double layer of foil and seal the foil to form a parcel. Preheat a barbecue flat plate to low–medium direct heat and grill the parcels for 6–8 minutes on each side or until they are heated through.

Unwrap the foil parcels and slide the tortillas onto serving plates. Top them with the sour cream, garnish with coriander sprigs and serve them with the lime wedges. Even better, add some guacamole (see page 334) and tomato salsa (see page 342).

Serves 4

Lebanese chicken

250 g (1 cup) plain Greek-style
   yoghurt
2 teaspoons soft brown sugar
4 garlic cloves, crushed
3 teaspoons ground cumin
1½ teaspoons ground coriander
7 g (¼ cup) chopped flat-leaf
   (Italian) parsley
60 ml (¼ cup) lemon juice
1 x 1.8 kg (4 lb) chicken, cut into
   10 serving pieces
cooking oil spray

Put the yoghurt, brown sugar, garlic, cumin, coriander, chopped parsley and lemon juice in a large non-metallic bowl and mix them together. Add the chicken pieces to the marinade and turn them so that they are completely coated, then cover and refrigerate for at least 2 hours, or overnight.

Lightly spray the barbecue plates with oil, then preheat the barbecue to medium direct heat. Take the chicken pieces out of the marinade and season them with salt and pepper. Cook the chicken pieces on the flat plate, turning them frequently, for 20–30 minutes, or until they are cooked through. If you have a barbecue with a lid, cover the barbecue while the chicken is cooking. This way, the breast pieces will take only 15 minutes to cook, while the pieces on the bone will take about 10 minutes longer. This dish is delicious served with eggplant, tomato and sumac salad (see page 301).

Serves 4–6

Pork with apple and onion wedges

2 pork fillets, about 400 g (14 oz)
  each
12 pitted prunes
2 green apples, cored, unpeeled,
  cut into wedges
2 red onions, cut into wedges
50 g (1¾ oz) butter, melted
2 teaspoons caster (superfine)
  sugar
125 ml (½ cup) cream
2 tablespoons brandy
1 tablespoon chopped chives

Trim the pork of any excess fat and sinew and cut each fillet in half. Make a slit with a knife through the centre of each fillet and push 3 prunes into each one. Brush the pork, the apple and onion wedges with the melted butter and sprinkle the apple and onion with the caster sugar.

Brown the pork on a hot, lightly oiled barbecue flat plate. Add the apple and onion wedges (you may need to cook in batches if your flat plate isn't large enough). Cook, turning frequently, for 5–7 minutes, or until the pork is cooked through and the apple and onion pieces are softened. Remove the pork, apple and onion from the barbecue and keep warm.

Mix together the cream, brandy and chives in a pan. Transfer to the stove top and simmer for 3 minutes, or until slightly thickened. Season with salt and black pepper.

Slice the meat and serve with the apple, onion wedges and brandy cream sauce.

Serves 4

Margarita chicken

4 chicken breasts, skin on, tenderloin
  and any excess fat removed
60 ml (¼ cup) tequila
60 ml (¼ cup) lime juice
2 small chillies, finely chopped
3 garlic cloves, crushed
15 g (¼ cup) finely chopped
  coriander (cilantro) leaves
1 tablespoon olive oil
lime wedges

Put the chicken, tequila, lime juice,
chilli, garlic, coriander and olive oil
in a non-metallic bowl and mix it all
together so that the chicken is coated
in the marinade. Cover the bowl and
refrigerate for at least 2 hours, or
preferably overnight.

Preheat a barbecue chargrill to
medium–high direct heat. Remove the
chicken breasts from the marinade,
season them with salt and pepper,
and grill for 7–8 minutes on each side
or until they are cooked through.

Slice the chicken breasts on the
diagonal and serve with lime wedges.
Delicious with avocado and grapefruit
salad (see page 322).

Serves 4

Rosemary and red wine steaks with barbecued vegetables

12 small new potatoes
60 ml (¼ cup) olive oil
1 tablespoon finely chopped
   rosemary
6 garlic cloves, sliced
sea salt flakes, to season
4 large, thick field mushrooms
12 asparagus spears
250 ml (1 cup) red wine
4 scotch fillet steaks (about 250 g/
   9 oz each)

Heat a barbecue plate or chargrill to hot. Toss the new potatoes with 1 tablespoon of oil, half the rosemary and half the garlic and season with the sea salt. Divide the potatoes among four large sheets of foil and wrap up into neat packages, sealing firmly around the edges. Place on the barbecue and cook, turning frequently for 30–40 minutes, or until tender. Meanwhile, brush the mushrooms and asparagus with a little oil and set aside.

Put the wine, remaining oil, rosemary and garlic in a non-metallic dish and season with pepper. Add the steaks and turn to coat well in the marinade. Leave for 25 minutes, then drain.

Place the steaks on the barbecue with the mushrooms and cook for 4 minutes each side, or until cooked to your liking. Transfer the steaks and mushrooms to a plate, cover lightly and allow to rest. Add the asparagus to the barbecue, turning regularly for about 2 minutes, or until tender. By this stage your potatoes should be cooked — open the foil and pierce with a skewer to check for doneness. Season with salt and pepper. Serve a steak per person, accompanied by a mushroom, three asparagus spears and a potato package.

Serves 4

Spanish-style seafood salad with romesco sauce

8 raw Balmain bugs (slipper lobsters)
1 kg (2 lb 4 oz) raw king prawns
    (jumbo shrimp)
500 g (1 lb 2 oz) baby squid tubes,
    cleaned
125 ml (½ cup) olive oil
3 garlic cloves, finely chopped
15 g (¼ cup) chopped basil
80 ml (⅓ cup) lemon juice
150 g (5½ oz) rocket (arugula)
    leaves
150 g (5½ oz) frisée lettuce
2 tablespoons extra virgin olive oil
1 tablespoon red wine vinegar

Romesco sauce
80 ml (⅓ cup) olive oil
¼ teaspoon paprika
1 small red capsicum (pepper),
    seeded and quartered lengthways
3 ripe Roma (plum) tomatoes
2 long red chillies
50 g (⅓ cup) blanched almonds
    and hazelnuts, toasted
3 garlic cloves, crushed
1 tablespoon red wine vinegar
1 tablespoon lemon juice

To prepare the bugs, cut into the membrane where the head and body join, then twist off the tail and discard the head. Use kitchen scissors to cut down both sides of the underside shell, working the scissors between the flesh and shell, then peel back the undershell and throw it away. Remove the heads and legs from the prawns, leaving the shells and tails intact. Turn each prawn on its back and cut a slit through the centre lengthways, taking care not to cut all the way through. Open out the prawn to form a butterfly and remove the dark vein from the back, starting at the head end. Wash the squid and pat them dry with paper towels, then cut a small slit in the base of the tubes so that they open up when cooking.

Mix together the oil, garlic, basil and lemon juice in a large bowl, add the seafood and toss so that it is well coated. Cover and chill for 30 minutes.

To make the romesco sauce, preheat a barbecue to medium direct heat. Mix half the olive oil with the paprika, add the capsicum, tomatoes and chillies, and toss. Cook the capsicum and tomatoes on the chargrill plate for 5 minutes, then add the chillies and cook for another 5 minutes or until the tomatoes are soft and the vegetables are charred. Peel the capsicum and

tomatoes when they are cool, then remove the seeds and skin from the chilli. Process the nuts until they are finely ground. Add the vegetables, garlic, vinegar and juice, and blend to a paste. Slowly add the remaining oil and season to taste. If the sauce is too thick, add 2 tablespoons of water to get it to a pouring consistency.

Toss the salad leaves with the olive oil and vinegar, cover and refrigerate.

Heat the barbecue chargrill plate to very high direct heat. Cook the bugs for 5–6 minutes, or until the shells turn pink and the flesh starts pulling away from the shells. Halfway through cooking the bugs, add the prawns and cook them, flesh-side down, for 2–3 minutes. Turn and cook for another 2–3 minutes, or until pink and cooked through. Add the squid after turning the prawns, and cook for 1–2 minutes, or until they are brown, marked and just cooked through. Remove all of the seafood from the barbecue as soon as it is just done, as residual heat will continue to cook it. Arrange the salad leaves on a plate, top with the seafood and drizzle with the romesco sauce. Serve at once, with any remaining romesco sauce and bread rolls to soak up the juices.

Serves 4

Lamb chops with citrus pockets

4 lamb chump chops, about 250 g
  (9 oz) each
2 tablespoons lemon juice

Citrus filling
3 spring onions (scallions), finely
  chopped
1 celery stalk, finely chopped
2 teaspoons grated fresh ginger
60 g (¾ cup) fresh breadcrumbs
2 tablespoons orange juice
2 teaspoons finely grated orange zest
1 teaspoon chopped rosemary

Cut a deep, long pocket in the side of each lamb chop. Mix together the spring onion, celery, ginger, breadcrumbs, orange juice, zest and rosemary and spoon into the pockets in the lamb.

Cook on a hot, lightly oiled barbecue flat plate or grill, turning once, for 15 minutes, or until the lamb is cooked through but still pink in the centre. Drizzle with the lemon juice before serving.

Serves 4

Five-spice roast chicken

1.8 kg (4 lb) chicken
1 tablespoon soy sauce
2 garlic cloves, crushed
1 teaspoon finely grated fresh ginger
1 tablespoon honey
1 tablespoon rice wine
1 teaspoon five-spice
1 tablespoon peanut oil

Wash the chicken and pat it thoroughly dry inside and out with paper towels. Whisk the soy sauce, garlic, ginger, honey, rice wine and five-spice together in a small bowl and brush it all over the chicken, ensuring every bit of skin is well coated. Put the chicken on a wire rack over a baking tray and refrigerate it, uncovered, for at least 8 hours, or overnight.

Preheat a kettle or covered barbecue to medium indirect heat and put a drip tray under the rack. Brush the chicken liberally with the peanut oil and put it breast-side up in the middle of the barbecue over the drip tray. Cover the barbecue and roast the chicken for 1 hour 10 minutes, or until the juices run clear when you pierce it with a skewer between the thigh and body. Check the chicken every so often, and if it appears to be over-browning, cover it loosely with foil. Leave it to rest, covered, for 10 minutes before carving and serving. The flavours in this style of chicken go particularly well with steamed Asian greens and fried rice.

Serves 4

Sweet chilli octopus

1.5 kg (3 lb 5 oz) baby octopus
250 ml (1 cup) sweet chilli sauce
80 ml (⅓ cup) lime juice
80 ml (⅓ cup) fish sauce
60 g (⅓ cup) soft brown sugar
lime wedges, to serve

Cut off the octopus heads, below the eyes, with a sharp knife. Discard the heads and guts. Push the beaks out with your index finger, remove and discard. Wash the octopus thoroughly under running water and drain on crumpled paper towels. If the octopus tentacles are large, cut into quarters.

Mix together the sweet chilli sauce, lime juice, fish sauce and sugar.

Cook the octopus on a very hot, lightly oiled barbecue grill or flat plate, turning often, for 3–4 minutes, or until it just changes colour. Brush with a quarter of the sauce during cooking. Take care not to overcook the octopus or it will toughen. Serve immediately with the remaining sauce and lime wedges.

Serves 4

Sesame and ginger beef

60 ml (¼ cup) sesame oil
60 ml (¼ cup) soy sauce
2 garlic cloves, crushed
2 tablespoons grated fresh ginger
1 tablespoon lemon juice
2 tablespoons chopped spring
  onions (scallions)
60 g (⅓ cup) soft brown sugar
500 g (1 lb 2 oz) beef fillet

Combine the sesame oil, soy sauce, garlic, ginger, lemon juice, spring onion and brown sugar in a non-metallic dish. Add the beef and coat well with the marinade. Cover and refrigerate for at least 2 hours, or overnight if possible.

Brown the beef on all sides on a very hot, lightly oiled barbecue grill or flat plate. When the beef is sealed, remove, wrap in foil and return to the barbecue, turning occasionally, for a further 15–20 minutes, depending on how well done you like your meat. Leave for 10 minutes before slicing.

Put the leftover marinade in a small saucepan and boil for 5 minutes. This is delicious served as a sauce with the beef.

Serves 4–6

Lobster with burnt butter sauce and grilled lemon

150 g (5½ oz) butter
60 ml (¼ cup) lemon juice
2 tablespoons chopped flat-leaf (Italian) parsley
1 small garlic clove, crushed
8 lobster tails in the shell
2 lemons, cut into wedges

Melt the butter in a small saucepan over medium heat and cook it for 3 minutes or until it begins to brown, but watch it carefully to make sure that it doesn't burn. Lower the heat, and cook the butter for another 2 minutes, or until it is a dark, golden brown. Remove the pan from the heat, add the lemon juice, parsley and garlic, and season with salt and freshly ground black pepper.

Cut the lobster tails lengthways and remove any digestive tract, but leave the meat in the shell. Preheat a barbecue chargrill plate to medium direct heat and brush the exposed lobster meat with lots of the butter mixture. Cook the lobster tails, cut-side down, on the chargrill plate for 6 minutes, then turn them over and cook for another 3–5 minutes, or until the shells turn bright red. While the lobster is cooking, put the lemon wedges on the hottest part of the chargrill and cook them for 1 minute on each side, or until they are marked and heated through. Arrange the lobster on a serving plate and serve it with the grilled lemon wedges and the rest of the warm brown butter as a dipping sauce. This is delicious with a green salad and some crusty bread to soak up the juices.

Serves 8

Lamb kofta with baba ganouj and grilled olives

Kofta
1 red onion, finely chopped
25 g (3/4 cup) chopped flat-leaf
  (Italian) parsley
25 g (1/2 cup) chopped coriander
  (cilantro) leaves
15 g (1/4 cup) chopped mint leaves
1 tablespoon paprika
1 tablespoon ground cumin
1 1/2 teaspoons allspice
1/2 teaspoon ground ginger
1/2 teaspoon chilli flakes
1.2 kg (2 lb 11 oz) minced (ground)
  lamb
60 ml (1/4 cup) soda water

Baba ganouj
2 (820 g/1 lb 12 oz) eggplants
  (aubergines)
2 garlic cloves, finely chopped
1/4 teaspoon ground cumin
60 ml (1/4 cup) lemon juice
2–2 1/2 tablespoons tahini
60 ml (1/4 cup) olive oil

1 tablespoon chopped flat-leaf
  (Italian) parsley
1/2 teaspoon sumac
200 g (7 oz) Kalamata olives
olive oil, for brushing
4 pieces pitta bread

To make the kofta, put the onion, parsley, coriander, mint, paprika, cumin, allspice, ginger and chilli in a food processor and blend until they are combined. Season the mixture with 2 teaspoons salt and some freshly ground black pepper, then add the minced lamb to the food processor and get the motor going again. Add the soda water in a thin stream until the mixture forms a smooth paste, then cover and refrigerate for at least 2 hours, or preferably overnight.

To make the baba ganouj, preheat a covered barbecue chargrill plate to medium–high. Prick the eggplants a few times with a fork and cook them, covered, for 20 minutes, or until they are soft and wrinkled, turning them halfway through the cooking time. Put the eggplants in a colander and leave them for 30 minutes to allow any bitter juices to drain, then peel and discard the skin and roughly chop the flesh. Put the eggplant in a food processor with the garlic, cumin, lemon juice, tahini and olive oil and process the baba ganouj for 30 seconds, or until it is smooth and creamy. Season to taste with salt, then cover and refrigerate it. Sprinkle the baba ganouj with the parsley and sumac before serving.

Soak four wooden skewers in cold water for 1 hour. Divide the lamb mixture into 12 portions and mould each portion into a torpedo shape, using damp hands to stop the meat from sticking to you, then cover and refrigerate the kofta. Thread the olives onto the soaked skewers.

When you're ready to cook the kofta, preheat a barbecue flat grill plate to medium–high direct heat. Brush the kofta lightly with olive oil and cook, turning frequently, for 10–12 minutes, or until they are evenly browned and cooked through. When the kofta are nearly cooked, add the olives to the barbecue for 1–2 minutes. Serve the kofta immediately with pitta bread, the baba ganouj and grilled olives. Tabbouleh (see page 305) makes a delicious accompaniment to this meal.

Serves 4

Spicy buffalo wings with ranch dressing

12 large chicken wings
2 teaspoons garlic salt
2 teaspoons onion powder
oil, for deep-frying
125 ml (½ cup) tomato sauce
2 tablespoons Worcestershire
  sauce
50 g (1¾ oz) butter, melted
Tabasco sauce, to taste

Ranch dressing
1 small garlic clove, crushed
185 g (¾ cup) mayonnaise
125 ml (½ cup) buttermilk
2 tablespoons finely chopped
  flat-leaf (Italian) parsley
1 tablespoon finely chopped
  chives
1½ teaspoons lemon juice
1½ teaspoons Dijon mustard
1 teaspoon onion powder

Pat the wings dry with paper towels, remove and discard the tip of each wing, then cut them in half at the joint. Combine the garlic salt, onion powder and 2 teaspoons of ground black pepper, and rub the spice mixture into each chicken piece.

Deep-fry the chicken in batches for 2–3 minutes without letting it brown, then remove from the oil and drain on crumpled paper towels. When the chicken has cooled a little, put it in a non-metallic bowl with the combined tomato sauce, Worcestershire sauce, butter and Tabasco, and toss so that all of the pieces are well coated in the marinade. Cover and refrigerate for at least 2 hours, or overnight.

To make the ranch dressing, mash the garlic and ¼ teaspoon salt to a paste then add the mayonnaise, buttermilk, parsley, chives, lemon juice, mustard and onion powder, and whisk it all together. Season well, cover and chill for at least 1 hour before serving.

Preheat a barbecue to medium direct heat. Cook the chicken for 6–8 minutes on each side, or until it is caramelized and sticky, turning and basting with the marinade as it cooks. Serve hot with the ranch dressing.

Serves 4

Adobo pork with coconut rice

170 ml (²/₃ cup) balsamic vinegar
80 ml (¹/₃ cup) soy sauce
3 fresh bay leaves
4 garlic cloves, crushed
6 pork loin chops on the bone
2 tablespoons oil
lime wedges

Coconut rice
400 g (2 cups) jasmine rice
2 tablespoons oil
1 small onion, finely diced
1 teaspoon grated fresh ginger
2 garlic cloves, crushed
625 ml (2¹/₂ cups) coconut milk

Put the balsamic vinegar, soy sauce, bay leaves, garlic and ¹/₂ teaspoon ground black pepper in a non-metallic dish and mix them all together. Add the pork chops to the marinade and turn them a few times so that they are thoroughly coated. Cover and chill for at least 3 hours, or overnight.

To make the coconut rice, rinse the rice under cold, running water until the water runs clear. Heat the oil in a heavy-based saucepan over medium heat, then add the onion, ginger and garlic. Cook for 3 minutes, or until the onion has softened, then add the rice and stir until the rice is coated in oil. Stir in the coconut milk, bring it to the boil, then turn the heat down as low as possible and cook it very gently, covered, for 15 minutes. Remove from the heat and let the rice sit with the lid on for 5 minutes, before gently fluffing it with a fork. Season well.

Preheat a barbecue chargrill plate to medium direct heat. Remove the pork from the marinade and pat it dry with paper towels. Brush both sides of the chops with oil, season and cook for 8 minutes each side, or until cooked through. Serve with the coconut rice and lime wedges. Delicious with grilled mango (see page 298).

Serves 6

Chicken with salsa verde

1 garlic clove
60 g (2 cups) fresh flat-leaf (Italian)
  parsley
80 ml (1/3 cup) extra virgin olive oil
3 tablespoons chopped dill
1 1/2 tablespoons Dijon mustard
1 tablespoon sherry vinegar
1 tablespoon baby capers, drained
6 large chicken breast fillets

Place the garlic, parsley, olive oil, dill, mustard, vinegar and capers in a food processor or blender and process until almost smooth.

Cook the chicken fillets on a very hot, lightly oiled barbecue grill or flat plate for 4–5 minutes each side, or until cooked through.

Cut each chicken fillet into three on the diagonal and arrange on serving plates. Top with a spoonful of salsa verde and season to taste.

Serves 6

Korean barbecue beef in lettuce leaves

600 g (1 lb 5 oz) sirloin steak
1 onion, grated
5 garlic cloves, crushed
125 ml (½ cup) Japanese soy sauce
1 teaspoon sesame oil
1 tablespoon oil
2 teaspoons finely grated fresh ginger
2 tablespoons soft brown sugar
1 tablespoon toasted sesame seeds, ground
1 butter lettuce
370 g (2 cups) cooked white rice
2 spring onions (scallions), finely sliced on the diagonal
2 small red chillies, sliced, or chilli sauce, optional

Trim any excess fat from the steak then put it in the freezer for about 45 minutes, or until it is almost frozen through. Put the onion, garlic, soy sauce, oils, ginger, sugar, ground sesame seeds and 1 teaspoon of freshly ground black pepper in a large, non-metallic bowl and stir it all together well.

Using a very sharp, heavy knife cut the steak across the grain into 2–3 mm (1/8 inch) thick slices. Use a meat mallet or rolling pin to pound the meat until it is as thin as possible. Add the meat to the marinade and stir it to make sure that all of the meat is well coated in the marinade. Cover and refrigerate overnight.

Separate the lettuce leaves and put them in a large bowl with enough cold water to cover them and refrigerate until ready to serve.

When you are ready to start cooking, remove the meat and the lettuce from the refrigerator and drain the lettuce well or dry it in a salad spinner. Put the lettuce leaves, hot rice, spring onion and chilli in separate bowls and put them on the table ready for each person to serve themselves. Preheat the flat plate to high indirect heat and, working quickly, put the beef strips on a barbecue flat plate, spacing them

out in a single layer, and cook them for about 10 seconds on each side. Do this in two batches if your barbecue isn't large enough to fit them all at once.

To make a wrap, put some rice in the bottom of a lettuce leaf, top it with a little meat, some spring onion and chilli if you like it, then wrap the leaf around the filling.

Serves 4–6

Squid with picada dressing

500 g (1 lb 2 oz) small squid

Picada dressing
2 tablespoons extra virgin olive oil
2 tablespoons finely chopped flat-leaf
  (Italian) parsley
1 garlic clove, crushed
¼ teaspoon cracked black pepper

To clean the squid, gently pull the tentacles away from the hood (the intestines should come away at the same time). Remove the intestines from the tentacles by cutting under the eyes, then remove the beak, if it remains in the centre of the tentacles, by pushing up with your index finger. Pull away the soft bone.

Rub the hoods under cold running water and the skin should come away easily. Wash the hoods and tentacles and drain well. Place in a bowl, add ¼ teaspoon salt and mix well. Cover and refrigerate for about 30 minutes.

For the picada dressing, whisk together the olive oil, parsley, garlic, pepper and some salt.

Cook the squid hoods in small batches on a very hot, lightly oiled barbecue flat plate for 2–3 minutes, or until white and tender. Barbecue or grill the squid tentacles, turning to brown them all over, for 1 minute, or until they curl up. Serve hot, drizzled with the picada dressing.

Serves 6

Tandoori lamb with tomato and onion salsa

60 g (¼ cup) tandoori paste
250 g (1 cup) thick plain yoghurt
1 tablespoon lemon juice
4 racks of lamb with 4–5 cutlets
  in each

Tomato and onion salsa
6 Roma (plum) tomatoes
1 red onion
2 tablespoons lemon juice
1 teaspoon sugar
2 tablespoons olive oil

Mix together the tandoori paste, yoghurt and the lemon juice in a large, non-metallic bowl. Trim any excess fat off the racks of lamb, add them to the marinade and turn them so that they are well coated. Cover and refrigerate for at least 4 hours, or overnight.

To make the tomato and onion salsa, cut the tomatoes into thin wedges, slice the onion very thinly and toss them both with the lemon juice, sugar and olive oil. Season the salsa with salt and lots of ground black pepper.

Preheat a kettle or covered barbecue to medium–high indirect heat. Cook the lamb, covered, for 10 minutes, then turn it, baste with the marinade and cook it for another 8 minutes. Leave it to rest, covered with foil, for 5 minutes. Serve the racks whole or sliced with the tomato salsa. This is delicious with minted potato salad (see page 326).

Serves 4

Drumsticks in tomato and mango chutney

8 chicken drumsticks, scored
1 tablespoon mustard powder
2 tablespoons tomato sauce
1 tablespoon sweet mango chutney
1 teaspoon Worcestershire sauce
1 tablespoon Dijon mustard
30 g (¼ cup) raisins
1 tablespoon oil

Toss the chicken in the mustard powder and season with salt and ground black pepper. Combine the tomato sauce, mango chutney, Worcestershire sauce, mustard, raisins and oil. Spoon over the chicken and toss well. Marinate for at least 2 hours, turning once.

Cook the chicken on a hot, lightly oiled barbecue flat plate for about 20 minutes, or until cooked through.

Serves 4

Smoked trout with lemon and dill butter

Lemon and dill butter
125 g (4½ oz) butter, softened
2 tablespoons lemon juice
2 tablespoons finely chopped dill
½ teaspoon lemon zest
1 small garlic clove, crushed

6 hickory woodchips
4 rainbow trout
oil, for brushing

Mash together the butter, lemon juice, dill, zest and garlic, shape it into a log and wrap it in greaseproof paper, twisting the ends to seal them. Refrigerate the butter until it is firm, then cut it into 1 cm (½ inch) slices and leave it at room temperature.

Preheat a kettle barbecue to low indirect heat, allow the coals to burn down to ash, then add three hickory woodchips to each side.

Brush the skin of the fish with oil. When the woodchips begin to smoke, put the trout on the barbecue, replace the cover and smoke them for 15 minutes or until they are cooked through. Remove the fish from the grill, gently peel off the skin and top them with the lemon and dill butter while they are still hot. Smoked trout are delicious with boiled new potatoes and a green salad, and can also be served cold.

Serves 4

Note: Like barbecuing, smoking is a simple process with a delicious result. Special woodchips are commercially available which will give off a wonderfully scented smoke and infuse your food with a distinctive flavour. Never use wood that is not specifically intended for smoking food, as many woods are chemically treated and may make the food poisonous. To smoke food, soak six woodchips in water for 1 hour and prepare a kettle barbecue for indirect cooking. When the briquettes are ready, add three woodchips to each side and close the lid until the chips begin to smoke, then cook the food according to the recipe, lifting the lid as little as possible so you don't lose too much of the smoke. Smoking does not work in a gas or electric barbecue as the chips need to burn to infuse their aromatic flavour.

Marinated vegetable salad with bocconcini and pesto dressing

2 large red capsicums (peppers), cored and seeded
5 slender eggplants (aubergines), cut into 1 cm ($\frac{1}{2}$ inch) slices on the diagonal
300 g (10$\frac{1}{2}$ oz) asparagus spears, trimmed and halved
4 zucchini (courgettes), cut into 1 cm ($\frac{1}{2}$ inch) slices on the diagonal
300 g (10$\frac{1}{2}$ oz) small field mushrooms, quartered
125 ml ($\frac{1}{2}$ cup) olive oil
4 garlic cloves, crushed
200 g (7 oz) bocconcini, sliced
150 g (5$\frac{1}{2}$ oz) baby rocket (arugula) leaves
1 tablespoon balsamic vinegar

Pesto
40 g (2 cups) small basil leaves
50 g ($\frac{1}{3}$ cup) pine nuts, toasted
3 garlic cloves, crushed
$\frac{1}{2}$ teaspoon sea salt
125 ml ($\frac{1}{2}$ cup) olive oil
20 g ($\frac{1}{2}$ oz) Parmesan cheese, finely grated
20 g ($\frac{1}{2}$ oz) pecorino cheese, finely grated

Cut the capsicums into quarters, then each quarter into three strips. Put the capsicum, eggplant, asparagus, zucchini and mushrooms in a large bowl, pour in the combined oil and garlic, season with salt and freshly ground pepper, and toss it all together. Leave the vegetables to marinate for 1 hour, tossing occasionally.

To make the pesto, put the basil, pine nuts, garlic, salt and oil in a food processor and process until it is smooth. Stir in the Parmesan and pecorino, then cover the bowl until you are ready to use it.

Heat a barbecue flat plate to high and cook the vegetables, turning, for about 7–8 minutes, or until they are soft and golden. Arrange the grilled vegetables on a serving plate with the bocconcini, and toss the rocket with the vinegar. Drizzle the vegetables with the pesto and serve them immediately with warmed, crusty bread rolls.

Serves 4

Thai spiced chicken with potato rosti

600 g (1 lb 5 oz) chicken breast fillet,
cut into strips
1 tablespoon chopped lemon grass
2 tablespoons lime juice
1½ tablespoons oil
2 garlic cloves, crushed
1 tablespoon grated fresh ginger
2 teaspoons sweet chilli sauce
2 spring onions (scallions), chopped
1 lime, cut into 6 wedges

Potato rosti
600 g (1 lb 5 oz) potatoes
3 tablespoons plain (all-purpose) flour
1 egg, lightly beaten

Remove any excess fat or sinew from the chicken and put the chicken in a shallow, non-metallic dish. Mix together the lemon grass, lime juice, oil, garlic, ginger, sweet chilli sauce and spring onion. Pour over the chicken pieces, cover and refrigerate for at least 2 hours.

To make the potato rosti, peel and grate the potatoes. Squeeze the excess moisture from the potato with your hands until it feels quite dry. Mix the potato with the flour and egg and season well. Divide into six equal portions. Cook on a hot, lightly oiled barbecue flat plate for 10 minutes, or until golden brown on both sides, flattening them down with the back of a spatula during cooking.

Drain the chicken and reserve the marinade. Cook on a barbecue grill or flat plate for 3 minutes each side, or until tender and golden brown. Brush with the reserved marinade while cooking. Serve with the rosti and a squeeze of lime juice.

Serves 6

Tuna steaks on coriander noodles

60 ml (¼ cup) lime juice
2 tablespoons fish sauce
2 tablespoons sweet chilli sauce
2 teaspoons grated palm sugar
1 teaspoon sesame oil
1 garlic clove, finely chopped
1 tablespoon virgin olive oil
4 tuna steaks (150 g/5½ oz each),
   at room temperature
200 g (7 oz) dried thin wheat noodles
6 spring onions (scallions), thinly
   sliced
25 g (¾ cup) chopped coriander
   (cilantro) leaves
lime wedges, to garnish

To make the dressing, place the lime juice, fish sauce, chilli sauce, sugar, sesame oil and garlic in a small bowl and mix together.

Heat the olive oil on a barbecue chargrill plate. Add the tuna steaks and cook over high heat for 2 minutes each side, or until cooked to your liking. Transfer the steaks to a warm plate, cover and keep warm.

Put the noodles in a large saucepan of lightly salted, rapidly boiling water and return to the boil. Cook for 4 minutes, or until the noodles are tender. Drain well. Add half the dressing and half the spring onion and coriander to the noodles and gently toss together.

Either cut the tuna into even cubes or slice it.

Place the noodles on serving plates and top with the tuna. Mix the remaining dressing with the spring onion and coriander and drizzle over the tuna. Garnish with lime wedges.

Serves 4

Roast sirloin with mustard pepper crust and hasselback potatoes

90 g (⅓ cup) Dijon mustard
2 tablespoons light soy sauce
2 tablespoons plain (all-purpose) flour
60 ml (¼ cup) olive oil
3 teaspoons chopped thyme leaves
4 garlic cloves, crushed
2.5 kg (5 lb 8 oz) piece of sirloin,
    trimmed but with the fat still on top
6 potatoes
2 tablespoons butter, melted
1 onion, roughly diced
1 large carrot, roughly diced
2 celery stalks, roughly chopped
250 ml (1 cup) red wine
500 ml (2 cups) beef stock
2 bay leaves
2 teaspoons cornflour (cornstarch)

Mix the mustard, soy sauce, flour, 2 tablespoons of oil, 2 teaspoons of thyme, two of the crushed garlic cloves and 1 tablespoon of cracked black pepper in a small bowl.

Coat the sirloin with the mustard mixture, put it on a wire rack over a tray and refrigerate it for 1 hour so the crust sets.

To make the hasselback potatoes, boil the potatoes in their skins for 10–12 minutes, or until they are just cooked. Once they are cool enough to handle, peel and cut them in half lengthways. Make small even slices across the top of the potato, cutting only two-thirds of the way down, brush each one liberally with butter and season them well with salt and ground pepper.

Heat the remaining olive oil in a large saucepan, add the onion, carrot, celery and remaining garlic, and cook them for 5 minutes. Pour in the red wine, cook for another 5 minutes, then add the beef stock, the bay leaves and the remaining thyme. Mix the cornflour with 1 tablespoon water until it is smooth and add it to the pan. Simmer the sauce over low heat for 20 minutes, or until it is slightly thickened, then strain and season to taste with salt and pepper.

Preheat a kettle or covered barbecue to medium indirect heat, put the sirloin in the middle of the barbecue and arrange the potatoes arround it. Replace the cover and cook for 45 minutes.

Remove the sirloin from the barbecue, and leave it to rest, covered, for about 10 minutes before carving. Serve the steak with the hasselback potatoes and red wine sauce. Delicious with chargrilled asparagus (see page 346).

Serves 6–8

Mirin and sake chicken

4 large chicken breast fillets
2 tablespoons mirin
2 tablespoons sake
1 tablespoon oil
5 cm (2 inch) piece of fresh ginger,
   very finely sliced
3 teaspoons soy sauce
salad leaves, to serve

Put the chicken in a non-metallic dish. Combine the mirin, sake and oil and pour over the chicken. Marinate for 15 minutes, then drain the chicken, reserving the marinade.

Cook the chicken on a hot, lightly oiled barbecue grill or flat plate for 4 minutes each side, or until tender.

Put the ginger in a pan and add the reserved marinade. Boil for about 7 minutes, or until thickened. Drizzle the soy sauce over the chicken and top with the ginger. Serve immediately on a bed of salad leaves.

Serves 4

Honey roasted pork fillet

1 tablespoon finely grated fresh
  ginger
6 garlic cloves
80 ml (⅓ cup) soy sauce
2 tablespoons oil
2 kg (4 lb 8 oz) piece pork neck
  or blade roast
2 tablespoons honey

Mix the ginger, garlic, soy sauce and oil in a large, non-metallic bowl. Put the pork in the marinade and turn it so that it is well coated, then cover the bowl and refrigerate it overnight.

Remove the pork from the marinade, pour the marinade into a small saucepan and simmer it over low heat for 5 minutes or until it is slightly reduced. Stir the honey into the warm marinade and remove it from the heat. Preheat a kettle or covered barbecue to low–medium indirect heat, then put the pork in the middle of the barbecue and roast it, covered, for 45 minutes or until it is cooked through. In the last 10 minutes of cooking, baste the roast all over with the reduced marinade. Be careful not to let any of the marinade splash onto the grill, as it may burn and stick. Remove the roast from the barbecue and put it on a tray, covered, to rest for 10 minutes.

Carve the roast and serve it with any pan juices left in the tray. Warm parsley carrots (see page 340) make the perfect accompaniment.

Serves 6–8

Bacon-wrapped chicken

2 tablespoons olive oil
2 tablespoons lime juice
¼ teaspoon ground coriander
6 chicken breast fillets
4 tablespoons fruit chutney
3 tablespoons chopped pecan nuts
6 rashers bacon

Mix together the olive oil, lime juice, coriander and salt and pepper. Using a sharp knife, cut a pocket in the thickest section of each fillet. Mix together the chutney and nuts. Spoon 1 tablespoon of the chutney mixture into each chicken breast pocket.

Turn the tapered ends of the fillets to the underside. Wrap a slice of bacon around each fillet to enclose the filling and secure with a toothpick.

Put the chicken parcels on a hot, lightly oiled barbecue grill or flat plate and cook for 5 minutes on each side, or until cooked through, turning once. Brush with the lime juice mixture several times during cooking and drizzle with any leftover lime juice mixture to serve

Serves 6

Note: This recipe also works well with prosciutto, which is an Italian equivalent of bacon.

Marinated lamb

15 g (½ cup) finely chopped
   flat-leaf (Italian) parsley
20 g (⅓ cup) finely chopped
   coriander (cilantro) leaves
4 garlic cloves, crushed
1 tablespoon paprika
1 teaspoon dried thyme
125 ml (½ cup) olive oil
60 ml (¼ cup) lemon juice
2 teaspoons ground cumin
4 x 250 g (9 oz) lamb rumps
   or pieces of tenderloin, trimmed

Mix the parsley, coriander, garlic, paprika, thyme, oil, lemon juice and 1½ teaspoons cumin together in a non-metallic dish. Score diagonal lines in the fat on the lamb pieces with a sharp knife, then put them in the marinade, turning so they are evenly coated. Cover and refrigerate for at least 2 hours or overnight.

Heat a barbecue flat plate to medium direct heat. Season the lamb to taste with white pepper, the remaining ½ teaspoon of cumin and some salt. Cook the rumps fat-side up for 3 minutes and then cook the other side for 2–3 minutes, making sure the fat is well cooked. Take the lamb off the barbecue as soon as it is done, cover it with foil and put it aside to rest for about 5 minutes before carving. This dish is delicious served with Moroccan spiced carrot salad (see page 313).

Serves 4

Chinese barbecue pork with pancakes

2 tablespoons sugar
2 tablespoons light soy sauce
2 tablespoons hoisin sauce
2 tablespoons dark soy sauce
2 tablespoons rice wine
2 tablespoons yellow bean paste
  (see Notes)
2 teaspoons sesame oil
1 teaspoon five-spice powder
2 garlic cloves, crushed
1 teaspoon finely grated fresh ginger
1 kg (2 lb 4 oz) pork fillet
1 tablespoon honey
24 Peking duck pancakes (see Notes)
1 cucumber, seeded and cut into
  8 cm x 5 mm (3 x ¼ inch) strips
4 spring onions (scallions), cut into
  8 cm x 5 mm (3 x ¼ inch) strips
125 ml (½ cup) plum sauce

Put the sugar, light soy sauce, hoisin sauce, dark soy sauce, rice wine, yellow bean paste, sesame oil, five-spice powder, garlic, ginger and ¼ teaspoon ground white pepper in a large, non-metallic bowl. Mix them together well, add the pork fillet and turn it until it is thoroughly coated in the marinade. Cover and refrigerate it for at least 2 hours, or preferably overnight.

Take the pork out of the refrigerator and allow it to come back to room temperature. Drain the marinade into a small saucepan, add the honey and simmer it over low heat for about 5 minutes, or until it has reduced slightly. Preheat a barbecue chargrill plate to medium direct heat and cook the pork fillet on the chargrill plate for 20 minutes, or until it is caramelized and cooked through, turning and basting it with the honey marinade mixture in the last 5–8 minutes of cooking. Allow the fillet to rest for 5 minutes before slicing.

Wrap the pancakes in foil and sit them on a warm place on the grill while the pork is resting so that they heat through without cooking or burning. Put the sliced pork and warm pancakes out with the rest of the fillings and let everyone make up their own pancake parcels by wrapping some sliced pork, cucumber, spring onion and plum sauce in a pancake.

Serves 6

Notes: Yellow bean paste is made from fermented yellow soy beans and is available from Asian grocery stores. Peking duck pancakes are available frozen from Asian grocery stores or from Chinese barbecue meat shops.

Roast beef with barbecue sauce

2 tablespoons paprika
1 tablespoon onion powder
1 tablespoon garlic powder
2 teaspoons sugar
1 teaspoon chilli powder
60 ml (¼ cup) oil
1.5 kg (3 lb 5 oz) piece beef fillet

Barbecue sauce
2 tablespoons oil
1 small onion, finely chopped
4 garlic cloves, crushed
½ teaspoon chilli flakes
1 tablespoon paprika
½ teaspoon smoked paprika
375 ml (1½ cups) tomato sauce
125 ml (½ cup) beer
60 ml (¼ cup) cider vinegar
80 ml (⅓ cup) soft brown sugar
2 tablespoons Dijon mustard
80 ml (⅓ cup) Worcestershire sauce

Mix the paprika, onion powder, garlic powder, sugar, chilli powder, 2 teaspoons ground black pepper, 2 teaspoons salt and the oil in a small bowl. Rub the mixture all over the beef fillet, then cover it with plastic wrap and refrigerate overnight.

To make the barbecue sauce, put the oil in a small saucepan over medium heat, add the onion, garlic and chilli flakes, and cook them for 5 minutes or until the onion is soft. Add the remaining ingredients and 60 ml (¼ cup) water, and let the sauce simmer over low heat for 20 minutes, or until it is slightly thickened. Season well and let it cool.

Preheat a kettle or covered barbecue to medium indirect heat. Put the beef fillet in the middle of the barbecue and cook, covered, for 40 minutes for rare beef. If you would like medium beef, roast for another 10 minutes.

Brush the barbecue sauce all over the beef fillet and cook it, covered, for another 10 minutes. Remove the beef from the barbecue, cover it loosely with foil and let it rest for 10 minutes before carving and serving it with the remaining barbecue sauce.

Serves 6

Barbecued tuna and white bean salad

400 g (14 oz) tuna steaks
1 small red onion, thinly sliced
1 tomato, seeded and chopped
1 small red capsicum (pepper),
  thinly sliced
2 x 400 g (14 oz) tins cannellini
  beans
2 garlic cloves, crushed
1 teaspoon chopped thyme
4 tablespoons finely chopped
  flat-leaf (Italian) parsley
1½ tablespoons lemon juice
80 ml (⅓ cup) extra virgin olive oil
1 teaspoon honey
100 g (4 handfuls) rocket (arugula)
  leaves

Place the tuna steaks on a plate, sprinkle with cracked black pepper on both sides, cover with plastic wrap and refrigerate until needed.

Combine the onion, tomato and capsicum in a large bowl. Rinse the cannellini beans under cold running water for 30 seconds, drain and add to the bowl with the garlic, thyme and 3 tablespoons of the parsley.

Place the lemon juice, oil and honey in a small saucepan, bring to the boil, then simmer, stirring, for 1 minute, or until the honey dissolves. Remove from the heat.

Cook the tuna on a hot, lightly oiled barbecue grill or flat plate for 1 minute on each side. The meat should still be pink in the middle. Slice into small cubes and combine with the salad. Toss with the warm dressing.

Arrange the rocket on a platter. Top with the salad, season well and toss with the remaining parsley.

Serves 4–6

Blackened Cajun spiced chicken

1½ tablespoons onion powder
1½ tablespoons garlic powder
2 teaspoons paprika
1 teaspoon white pepper
2 teaspoons dried thyme
½–1 teaspoon chilli powder
8 chicken drumsticks, scored

Combine the onion powder, garlic powder, paprika, white pepper, thyme, chilli powder and 1 teaspoon salt in a plastic bag. Place the drumsticks in the bag and shake until all the pieces are coated. Leave the chicken in the fridge for at least 30 minutes to allow the flavours to develop, or overnight if time permits.

Cook the chicken on a lightly oiled barbecue grill for 55–60 minutes, or until slightly blackened and cooked through. Brush lightly with some oil to prevent drying out during cooking.

Serves 4

Fillet steak with flavoured butters

4 fillet steaks

Capsicum butter
1 small red capsicum (pepper)
125 g (4½ oz) butter
2 teaspoons chopped oregano
2 teaspoons chopped chives

Garlic butter
125 g (4½ oz) butter
3 garlic cloves, crushed
2 spring onions (scallions), finely
  chopped

Cut a pocket in each steak.

For the capsicum butter, cut the capsicum into large pieces and place, skin-side up, under a hot grill until the skin blisters and blackens. Put in a plastic bag until cool, then peel away the skin and dice the flesh. Beat the butter until creamy. Add the capsicum, oregano and chives, season and beat until smooth.

For the garlic butter, beat the butter until creamy, add the garlic and spring onion and beat until smooth.

Push capsicum butter into the pockets in two of the steaks and garlic butter into the other two. Cook on a hot, lightly oiled barbecue grill or flat plate for 4–5 minutes each side, turning once. Brush frequently with any remaining flavoured butter while cooking. These steaks are delicious served with a simple green salad.

Serves 4

Roast rack of pork with chunky apple sauce and vegetables

6 Granny Smith apples
90 g (⅓ cup) sugar
60 ml (¼ cup) white vinegar
2 tablespoons finely shredded
   mint leaves
1 rack of pork with 6 ribs (about
   1.6 kg/3 lb 8 oz)
1 tablespoon olive oil

Roasted vegetables
2 orange sweet potatoes
1 kg (2 lb 4 oz) piece pumpkin
12 small onions
6 carrots
80 ml (⅓ cup) olive oil
6 garlic cloves, unpeeled
2 tablespoons finely chopped
   flat-leaf (Italian) parsley

Peel the apples, remove the seeds, and roughly dice the flesh. Simmer them over low heat with the sugar, vinegar and 60 ml (¼ cup) water in a small saucepan for 15 minutes, or until they are cooked through and just beginning to collapse. Remove the sauce from the heat and stir in the shredded mint.

Score the skin on the rack of pork in a large diamond pattern, rub the oil all over the pork, then rub 1 teaspoon salt into the skin. To make the roast vegetables, peel the sweet potatoes, pumpkin, onions and carrots, and cut them into large, even pieces. Toss the vegetables with 2 tablespoons of olive oil until they are coated, and season them well with salt and freshly ground black pepper. Trim the root end from the garlic cloves, drizzle ½ teaspoon of oil over them and wrap them in a double layer of foil.

Preheat a kettle or covered barbecue to medium indirect heat. Put the pork rack in the middle of the barbecue, cover it and roast for about 1 hour 20 minutes, or until the juices run clear when a skewer is inserted into the thickest part of the flesh. When the pork has been cooking for about 20 minutes, arrange the vegetables around the roast and cook them, covered, for 1 hour or until they are golden and tender. Add the garlic to the barbecue and cook it for 30 minutes or until it has softened.

When the garlic cloves are cool enough to handle, squeeze them from their skin, mash them with the remaining olive oil and stir in the chopped parsley. Season with salt and ground pepper, and drizzle the dressing over the roast vegetables just before serving.

When the pork is cooked, remove it from the barbecue, and leave it to rest, covered, for 10 minutes. Slice between the bones and serve it with the roasted vegetables and chunky apple sauce.

Serves 6

Honey mustard chicken

175 g (½ cup) honey
60 g (¼ cup) Dijon mustard
2 tablespoons oil
2 tablespoons white wine vinegar
3 garlic cloves, crushed
2 tablespoons chopped parsley
  leaves
1.8 kg (4 lb) chicken, cut into
  10 serving pieces

Put the honey, mustard, oil, white wine vinegar, garlic, parsley and ¼ teaspoon freshly ground black pepper in a large, non-metallic bowl. Mix it all together well, and put aside 60 ml (¼ cup) of the marinade to baste the chicken during cooking. Add the chicken pieces to the rest of the marinade and turn them so that they are thoroughly coated. Cover the bowl and refrigerate it for at least 4 hours, or overnight.

Preheat a covered or kettle barbecue to medium indirect heat and cook the chicken pieces for 20–30 minutes, or until they are cooked through. The breast pieces may take as little as 15 minutes, while dark meat will take longer. Baste the chicken with the reserved marinade during the last 5–8 minutes of cooking, but no earlier or it is likely to burn. The chicken is delicious served on a bed of spring onion mash (see page 310).

Serves 4–6

Stuffed baby calamari with lime and chilli dipping sauce

Dipping sauce
80 ml (1/3 cup) lime juice
60 ml (1/4 cup) fish sauce
2 tablespoons grated palm sugar
  or soft brown sugar
1 small red chilli, finely sliced into
  rounds

12 medium squid
12 raw prawns (shrimp), peeled,
  deveined and chopped
150 g (5 1/2 oz) minced (ground) pork
4 garlic cloves, crushed
1/2 teaspoon finely grated fresh
  ginger
3 teaspoons fish sauce
2 teaspoons lime juice
1 teaspoon grated palm sugar
2 tablespoons chopped coriander
  (cilantro) leaves
peanut oil, for brushing

For the dipping sauce, put the lime juice, fish sauce, palm sugar and chilli in a bowl and stir it together until the sugar has dissolved. Cover the bowl.

Gently pull the tentacles away from the tube of the squid (the intestines should come away at the same time). Remove the quill from inside the body and discard, as well as any white membrane. Pull the skin away from the hood under running water, then cut the tentacles away from the intestines and give them a rinse to remove the sucker rings. Finely chop the tentacles to add to the stuffing.

Put the prawns, pork, garlic, ginger, fish sauce, juice, sugar, coriander and chopped tentacles in a bowl and mix together. Use a teaspoon to put the stuffing in each tube and push it to the bottom, then secure the hole with a toothpick. Don't overfill the tubes as the stuffing will expand when cooked.

Preheat the chargrill plate to medium direct heat, brush the squid tubes with peanut oil, and barbecue them for 8 minutes, or until cooked, turning when the flesh becomes opaque and slightly charred. Remove the tooth-picks and cut each tube into thin rounds. Serve with the dipping sauce.

Serves 4

Fennel and pork sausages with onion relish

750 g (1 lb 10 oz) minced (ground) pork
40 g (½ cup) fresh breadcrumbs
2 garlic cloves, crushed
3 teaspoons fennel seeds, coarsely crushed
1 teaspoon finely grated orange zest
2 teaspoons chopped thyme leaves
7 g (¼ cup) chopped flat-leaf (Italian) parsley
oil, for brushing
1 long baguette, cut into 4 pieces, or 4 long, crusty rolls
50 g (1¾ oz) butter, softened
60 g (2¼ oz) rocket (arugula) leaves
1 tablespoon extra virgin olive oil
1 teaspoon balsamic vinegar

Onion relish
50 g (1¾ oz) butter
2 red onions, thinly sliced
1 tablespoon soft brown sugar
2 tablespoons balsamic vinegar

Put the pork, breadcrumbs, garlic, fennel seeds, zest, thyme and parsley in a large bowl, season well with salt and freshly ground black pepper and mix it all together with your hands. Cover the mixture and refrigerate it for 4 hours or overnight.

To make the onion relish, melt the butter in a heavy-based saucepan, add the onion and cook, stirring occasionally, over low heat for about 10 minutes, or until the onion is softened, but not browned. Add the sugar and vinegar, and continue to cook for another 30 minutes, stirring regularly.

Preheat a barbecue flat plate to medium direct heat. Divide the pork mixture into eight portions and use wet hands to mould each portion into a flattish sausage shape. Lightly brush the sausages with oil and cook them for 8 minutes on each side, or until they are cooked through.

To assemble, split the rolls down the middle and butter them. Toss the rocket with the olive oil and balsamic vinegar, and put some of the leaves in each of the rolls. Top with a sausage and some of the onion relish.

Makes 8

Rosemary lamb on grilled polenta with anchovy sauce

600 g (1 lb 5 oz) lamb fillets
1 tablespoon finely chopped
  rosemary leaves
3 garlic cloves, bruised
2 tablespoons olive oil
1 tablespoon lemon juice
250 g (1$^2/_3$ cups) instant polenta
35 g ($^1/_3$ cup) grated Parmesan
  cheese
20 g ($^1/_2$ oz) butter
60 g (1$^1/_2$ cups) rocket (arugula)
  leaves

Anchovy and rosemary sauce
8 large anchovy fillets, chopped
3 teaspoons finely chopped
  rosemary leaves
150 ml (5$^1/_2$ fl oz) olive oil
1 tablespoon lemon juice

Trim the lamb fillets of any fat and sinew, and put them in a non-metallic bowl with the rosemary, garlic, olive oil and lemon juice, turning the fillets until they are well coated. Season with pepper, cover the bowl and refrigerate it for at least 4 hours, or preferably overnight.

Meanwhile, to make the polenta, bring 1 litre of salted water to the boil in a heavy-based saucepan. Whisking constantly, add the polenta in a thin stream and stir until it thickens and starts to come away from the side of the pan. Remove the pan from the heat and add the Parmesan and butter, then season generously with salt and freshly ground black pepper. Stir the polenta until the cheese and butter have melted, then pour it into a lightly greased 22 cm (9 inch) square baking tin and smooth the surface. Refrigerate the polenta for 2 hours or until it is cool and firm, then turn it out onto a chopping board, trim the edges and cut the block into four squares.

While the polenta is cooling, make the anchovy and rosemary sauce. Put the anchovies and rosemary in a food processor and blend them to a paste. Add the olive oil in a thin stream, then add the lemon juice and season with salt and pepper.

Preheat a barbecue chargrill plate to medium direct heat. Grill the polenta squares for 7–8 minutes on each side or until they are crisp and golden. When the polenta is ready, move the squares to the side of the grill, season the lamb fillets with salt and cook for 2–3 minutes each side for medium–rare, or until cooked to your liking.

To serve, slice the lamb fillets into four pieces on the diagonal, cutting across the grain. Put the grilled polenta on warmed serving plates, top it with the lamb and rocket and drizzle with the sauce.

Serves 4

Lemon and sage marinated veal chops with rocket

4 veal chops
2 tablespoons olive oil
1 tablespoon lemon juice
4 strips lemon zest
10 g (¼ cup) roughly chopped sage
  leaves
3 garlic cloves, peeled and bruised
lemon wedges, to serve

Rocket salad
100 g (3½ oz) rocket (arugula),
  washed and picked
1 avocado, sliced
1½ tablespoons extra virgin olive oil
2 teaspoons balsamic vinegar

Trim any fat and sinew from the chops and put them in a shallow, non-metallic dish with the olive oil, lemon juice, lemon zest, sage and garlic. Turn the chops so that they are evenly coated, then season them with freshly ground black pepper, cover and refrigerate for 4 hours or preferably overnight.

Put the rocket in a large serving bowl and scatter the avocado over it. Drizzle the olive oil and balsamic vinegar over the salad, season it with a little salt and ground black pepper and toss gently.

Preheat a barbecue chargrill plate to medium–high direct heat. Remove the chops from the marinade, season well with salt and chargrill them for 5–6 minutes on each side, or until cooked to your liking. Remove the chops from the barbecue, cover them loosely with foil and let them rest for 5 minutes.

Put the chops on a serving dish, drizzle them with any juices that have been released while they rested and serve with the rocket salad and lemon wedges.

Serves 4

Chinese-style barbecue spareribs

60 ml (¼ cup) hoisin sauce
80 ml (⅓ cup) oyster sauce
2 tablespoons rice wine
125 ml (½ cup) soy sauce
6 garlic cloves, crushed
3 teaspoons finely grated fresh
  ginger
2 kg (4 lb 8 oz) American-style
  pork ribs
2 tablespoons honey

Mix the hoisin sauce, oyster sauce, rice wine, soy sauce, garlic and ginger in a large, non-metallic bowl, add the ribs and turn them so that they are coated in the marinade. Cover the bowl and refrigerate for at least 4 hours, or overnight.

Remove the ribs from the marinade and tip the marinade into a small saucepan with the honey. Simmer the mixture over low heat for 5 minutes, or until it becomes slightly syrupy — you will be using this to baste the ribs as they cook.

Heat a kettle or covered barbecue to medium indirect heat and cook the ribs, covered, for 10 minutes, then turn them over and cook them for another 5 minutes. Continue cooking, basting and turning the ribs frequently for 30 minutes, or until they are cooked through and caramelized all over.

Once the ribs are cooked, let them rest, covered, for 10 minutes, then cut the racks into individual ribs to serve. Make sure there are plenty of napkins available — these ribs should be eaten with your fingers and are deliciously sticky.

Serves 6

Teriyaki baby octopus

125 ml (½ cup) sake
125 ml (½ cup) mirin
125 ml (½ cup) dark soy sauce
1 tablespoon caster (superfine) sugar
2 teaspoons grated fresh ginger
2 garlic cloves, finely chopped
1 kg (2 lb 4 oz) baby octopus

Combine the sake, mirin, dark soy sauce and sugar in a small saucepan. Bring the mixture to the boil over medium heat and boil, stirring until all the sugar has dissolved, then add the ginger and garlic and remove the saucepan from the heat. Leave the mixture to cool for 30 minutes.

To prepare the octopus, use a small knife to carefully cut between the head and tentacles of the octopus, just below the eyes. Push the beak out and up through the tentacles with your finger, then remove the eyes from the head of the octopus by cutting off a small disc and discarding it. To clean the octopus tube, carefully slit through one side, avoiding the ink sac, and scrape out any gut. Rinse the inside under running water to remove any remaining gut and cut it in half. Wash the rest of the octopus thoroughly under running water, pulling the skin away from the tube and tentacles. If the octopus are large, cut the tentacles into quarters.

Put the octopus in a large, non-metallic bowl. Whisk the teriyaki marinade, making sure that it is well combined, then pour it over the octopus, stirring so that the octopus is thoroughly coated. Cover and marinate it in the refrigerator for at least 2 hours, or overnight.

Preheat a barbecue chargrill plate to medium direct heat. Remove the octopus from the teriyaki marinade and cook them for 2–3 minutes, or until they are cooked through, curled and glazed. Delicious served on a bed of Asian salad (see page 345).

Serves 4

Sides

Pear and walnut salad

60 ml (¼ cup) walnut oil
1¼ tablespoons sherry vinegar
1 teaspoon Dijon mustard
3 ripe pears, halved, cored and cut
    into 1 cm (½ inch) thick wedges
50 g (1¾ oz) butter, melted
1 tablespoon soft brown sugar
2 heads witlof (chicory/Belgian
    endive), leaves separated
85 g (⅔ cup) walnut pieces,
    toasted, chopped

To make the salad dressing, whisk the walnut oil, vinegar, mustard and some freshly ground black pepper in a bowl. Put the pears, melted butter and sugar in a bowl and toss them together until the pears are well coated in the butter.

Cook the pear slices on a barbecue flat plate preheated to medium–high for 1 minute each side or until they are golden and slightly caramelized, basting with the butter and sugar mixture during cooking.

Put the witlof in a large bowl, add the dressing, walnuts and pears, toss well and serve.

Serves 4

Grilled mango

3 small mangoes
2 teaspoons oil

Preheat a barbecue to medium direct heat. To prepare the mango, cut each cheek straight down on either side of the stone. Score the flesh without cutting through the skin and lightly brush the cut surface with the oil.

Cook the mango on the chargrill plate, skin-side down, for 2 minutes, then turn it 90 degrees and cook for another 2 minutes to make crossed grill marks. Serve warm.

Serves 4–6

Eggplant, tomato and sumac salad

2 eggplants (aubergines), cut into
1 cm (½ inch) thick rounds
100 ml (3½ fl oz) olive oil
5 large ripe tomatoes
1 small red onion, finely sliced
20 g (⅓ cup) roughly chopped
mint leaves
10 g (⅓ cup) roughly chopped
flat-leaf (Italian) parsley
2 teaspoons sumac (see Note)
2 tablespoons lemon juice

Put the eggplant slices in a colander, and sprinkle them with salt. Leave the eggplant for 30 minutes to allow some of the bitter juices to drain away, then rinse the slices and pat them dry with paper towels. Using 2 tablespoons of the olive oil, brush both sides of each slice, then chargrill them for 5 minutes on each side or until they are cooked through. Let the slices cool slightly and cut them in half.

Cut the tomatoes into wedges and arrange them in a serving bowl with the eggplant and onion. Scatter the mint, parsley and sumac over the top, then put the lemon juice and remaining olive oil in a small, screw-top jar, season, and shake it up. Drizzle the dressing over the salad and toss it gently.

Serves 6

Note: Sumac is a spice made from crushing the dried sumac berry. It has a mild lemony flavour and is used extensively in many cuisines, from North Africa and the Middle East, to India and Asia.

Chargrilled potatoes with pistachio salsa

Pistachio salsa
150 g (5½ oz) pistachio nuts, toasted
2 ripe tomatoes, chopped
2 garlic cloves, finely chopped
1 small red chilli, finely chopped
2 tablespoons chopped flat-leaf
  (Italian) parsley
1 tablespoon chopped mint
1 teaspoon finely grated lemon zest

750 g (1 lb 10 oz) potatoes
3 tablespoons plain (all-purpose) flour
2 tablespoons olive oil
sour cream, to serve

To make the pistachio salsa, roughly chop the nuts and combine with the tomato, garlic, chilli, herbs and lemon zest. Season with salt and pepper.

Peel the potatoes and cut into large wedges. Place in a pan and cover with water, bring to the boil and cook for 5 minutes. Transfer to a colander and rinse under running water to stop the cooking. Pat the wedges dry with paper towels.

Sprinkle the flour over the potatoes in a bowl and toss to lightly coat. Cook the potato wedges in a single layer on a hot, lightly oiled barbecue flat plate or grill for 5–10 minutes, or until golden brown and tender. Drizzle with the olive oil and turn the potatoes regularly during cooking. Serve with the salsa and a bowl of sour cream.

Serves 4

Tabbouleh

130 g (³/₄ cup) burghul (bulgar)
3 ripe tomatoes
1 telegraph (long) cucumber
80 ml (⅓ cup) lemon juice
60 ml (¼ cup) olive oil
1 tablespoon extra virgin olive oil
4 spring onions (scallions), sliced
120 g (4 cups) chopped flat-leaf
   (Italian) parsley
10 g (¼ oz) chopped mint

Place the burghul in a bowl, cover with 500 ml (2 cups) water and leave it for 1½ hours. Cut the tomatoes in half, squeeze the halves gently to remove any excess seeds and cut the flesh into 5 mm (¼ inch) cubes. Cut the cucumber in half lengthways, remove the seeds and cut the flesh into 5 mm (¼ inch) cubes. Drain the burghul, squeezing out any excess water, and spread it out across a clean tea towel for 30 minutes to dry.

Whisk together the lemon juice and 1½ teaspoons of salt until they are well combined. Season the dressing with pepper, then slowly whisk in the olive oil and extra virgin olive oil. Put the burghul in a large bowl and add the tomato, cucumber, spring onion, parsley and mint. Toss the dressing with the tabbouleh, then cover and refrigerate.

Serves 4–6

Smoky tomato sauce

Smoking mix
2 tablespoons Chinese or Ceylon
  tea leaves
2 star anise, crushed
1 strip orange zest
½ teaspoon five-spice powder
6 juniper berries, crushed

2 onions, quartered
2 red capsicums (peppers), cut into
  large pieces
2 red chillies, cut in half
3 tablespoons oil
3 garlic cloves, chopped
500 g (1 lb 2 oz) tomatoes, chopped
2 tablespoons Worcestershire sauce
125 ml (½ cup) barbecue sauce
2 tablespoons tamarind concentrate
1 tablespoon white vinegar
1 tablespoon soft brown sugar

Combine all the ingredients for the smoking mix in a bowl. Pour the mix into the centre of a sheet of foil and fold the edges to prevent spreading. (This will form an open container to allow the mix to smoke.) Place the foil container on the bottom of a dry wok or wide frying pan. Put an open rack or steamer in the wok or frying pan, making sure it is elevated over the mix.

Place the onion, capsicum and chilli on the rack and cover with a lid, or alternatively cover the entire wok or frying pan tightly with foil to prevent the smoke from escaping.

Smoke over medium heat for about 10–15 minutes, or until the vegetables are tender. For a very smoky sauce cook the vegetables for longer; if you prefer it less so, reduce the time. Remove the smoking mix container.

Dice the onion, capsicum and chilli quite finely. Heat the oil in the wok and add the garlic and cooked vegetables. Fry over medium heat for 3 minutes, then add the tomato and cook until pulpy. Add the sauces, tamarind, vinegar and sugar. Simmer, stirring occasionally, for about 20–25 minutes, or until the sauce is quite thick. Store in the refrigerator.

Makes about 1 litre

Fennel salad

2 large fennel bulbs
1 tablespoon lemon juice
1 tablespoon extra virgin olive oil
2 teaspoons red wine vinegar
150 g (5½ oz) Niçoise olives, pitted

Trim the fennel bulbs, reserving the fronds, and discard the tough outer layers. Using a very sharp knife, slice the fennel lengthways as thinly as possible and put it in a bowl of very cold water with the lemon juice.

Just before you are ready to serve the main meal, drain the fennel well, pat it dry with paper towels and toss it in a bowl with the olive oil and red wine vinegar. Finely chop the fennel fronds, add them to the fennel with the olives and season to taste with freshly ground black pepper.

Serves 4

Spring onion mash

1 kg (2 lb 4 oz) floury (starchy)
  potatoes
2 tablespoons butter
80 ml (⅓ cup) milk
60 ml (¼ cup) cream
3 spring onions (scallions),
  finely sliced

Peel the potatoes and cut them into large chunks. Steam or boil the pieces for 12 minutes, or until they are tender, then drain the water away and briefly return the potato to the heat, shaking the pan, to dry any excess moisture.

Add the butter, milk and cream, and mash the potato until it is smooth and lump-free. Stir in the spring onion, season to taste and serve warm.

Serves 4–6

Moroccan spiced carrot salad

4 carrots, peeled, trimmed and
  halved on the diagonal
80 ml (⅓ cup) olive oil
2 teaspoons ground cumin
95 g (½ cup) Kalamata olives, pitted
  and halved lengthways
5 g (¼ cup) flat-leaf (Italian) parsley
½–1 teaspoon harissa
2 tablespoons extra virgin olive oil
1 tablespoon red wine vinegar

Bring a saucepan of salted water to the boil and blanch the carrots for 3 minutes, or until they just begin to soften. Drain well, pat dry with paper towels, then toss them with 2 tablespoons of the olive oil and 1 teaspoon of the cumin. Cook the carrots on a hot griddle or barbecue plate for 25 minutes, turning them once so they are cooked through and golden all over.

While the carrots are still warm, cut them into thin diagonal slices and toss them with the olives and parsley. Mix the harissa with 1 tablespoon of water, add the extra virgin olive oil, red wine vinegar, remaining olive oil and remaining cumin, and whisk it together. Pour the dressing over the salad and season to taste with salt and pepper. Serve warm.

Serves 4

Barbecued corn in the husk

8 fresh young corn cobs
125 ml (½ cup) olive oil
6 garlic cloves, chopped
4 tablespoons chopped flat-leaf
  (Italian) parsley
butter, to serve

Peel back the corn husks, leaving them intact. Pull off the white silks, then wash the corn and pat dry with paper towels.

Combine the olive oil, garlic, parsley and some salt and black pepper and brush over each cob. Pull up the husks and tie together at the top with string. Steam over boiling water for 5 minutes, then pat dry.

Cook on a hot, lightly oiled barbecue grill or flat plate for 20 minutes, turning regularly. Spray with water during the cooking to keep the corn moist. Serve hot with knobs of butter.

Serves 8

Asian rice salad

400 g (2 cups) long-grain rice
2 tablespoons olive oil
1 large red onion, finely chopped
4 garlic cloves, crushed
1 tablespoon finely chopped fresh
  ginger
1 long red chilli, seeded and thinly
  sliced
4 spring onions (scallions), finely
  sliced
2 tablespoons soy sauce
½ teaspoon sesame oil
2 teaspoons black vinegar
  (see Note)
1 tablespoon lime juice
50 g (1 cup) roughly chopped
  coriander (cilantro) leaves

Bring 1.25 litres (5 cups) of water to
the boil in a large saucepan. Add
the rice and cook it, uncovered, for
12–15 minutes over low heat, or until
the grains are tender. Drain and rinse
the rice under cold running water,
then transfer it to a large bowl.

While the rice is cooking, heat the
oil in a frying pan over medium heat.
Add the onion, garlic, ginger and chilli,
and cook them for 5–6 minutes, or
until the onion has softened, but not
browned. Stir in the spring onion and
cook for another minute. Remove
the onion mixture from the heat and
add it to the rice with the soy sauce,
sesame oil, vinegar, lime juice and
coriander, and mix well. Cover the
rice salad and refrigerate until you
are ready to serve.

Serves 4

Note: Black vinegar is a type of
Chinese vinegar and can be found
in Asian grocery stores.

Pineapple mint salsa

1 small ripe pineapple
1 tablespoon grated palm sugar or
   soft brown sugar
1 small red chilli, seeded and finely
   diced
½ teaspoon rice vinegar
2 tablespoons lime juice
4 spring onions (scallions), finely
   chopped
15 g (¼ cup) chopped mint leaves

Peel the pineapple, remove all of the eyes and slice it lengthways into quarters. Remove the central core and cut the flesh into 1 cm (½ inch) dice. Put the pineapple in a non-metallic mixing bowl with the sugar, chilli, rice vinegar, lime juice, spring onion and mint and stir them together. Cover the bowl and refrigerate for 1 hour to let the flavours develop.

Serves 4

Red capsicum relish

1 kg (2 lb 4 oz) red capsicums
(peppers)
1 teaspoon black peppercorns
2 teaspoons black mustard seeds
2 red onions, thinly sliced
4 garlic cloves, chopped
375 ml (1½ cups) red wine vinegar
2 apples, peeled, cored and grated
1 teaspoon grated fresh ginger
185 g (1 cup) soft brown sugar

Remove the capsicum seeds and membrane and thinly slice. Tie the peppercorns in a piece of muslin and secure with string. Combine the capsicum, peppercorns, mustard seeds, onion, garlic, vinegar, apple and ginger in a large pan. Simmer, covered, for 30 minutes until the capsicum is soft.

Add the sugar and stir over low heat until completely dissolved. Cover and simmer, stirring occasionally, for 1¼ hours, or until the relish has reduced and thickened. Remove the muslin bag.

Rinse the jars with boiling water then dry in a warm oven. Spoon the relish into the hot jars and seal. Turn the jars upside down for 2 minutes, then turn them the other way up and leave to cool. Label and date. Leave for a few weeks before using. Will keep in a cool dark place for 1 year. Refrigerate after opening.

Fills three 1 cup (250 ml) jars

Avocado and grapefruit salad

2 ruby grapefruit
1 ripe avocado
200 g (7 oz) watercress leaves
1 French shallot, finely sliced
1 tablespoon sherry vinegar
60 ml (¼ cup) olive oil

Peel and segment the grapefruit, working over a bowl to save any juice drips for the dressing. Cut the avocado into 2 cm (¾ inch) wedges and put it in a bowl with the watercress, grapefruit and shallot.

Put 1 tablespoon of the reserved grapefruit juice in a small, screw-top jar with the sherry vinegar, olive oil, salt and black pepper, and shake it up. Pour the dressing over the salad and toss it gently.

Serves 4

Chargrilled cauliflower salad with tahini dressing and gremolata

Tahini dressing
65 g (¼ cup) tahini
1 garlic clove, crushed
60 ml (¼ cup) rice vinegar
1 tablespoon oil
¼ teaspoon sesame oil
1 teaspoon lemon juice

2 teaspoons sesame seeds, toasted
1 tablespoon finely chopped flat-leaf
   (Italian) parsley
½ small garlic clove, finely chopped
½ teaspoon finely grated lemon zest
1 cauliflower (about 1.8 kg/4 lb)
2 tablespoons oil
2 baby cos (romaine) lettuces,
   washed and drained
50 g (1¾ oz) watercress leaves,
   washed and drained

To make the dressing, whisk the tahini, garlic, rice vinegar, oils, lemon juice and 1 tablespoon of water together and season it to taste. Stir the sesame seeds, parsley, garlic and lemon zest together.

Divide the cauliflower into large florets and cut each floret into 1 cm (½ inch) thick slices. Brush the slices with oil and season well. Preheat a barbecue chargrill plate to medium direct heat and chargrill the cauliflower pieces for 6–8 minutes, or until they are cooked and golden on both sides.

Arrange the lettuce leaves and watercress on a serving dish and top them with the chargrilled cauliflower slices. Drizzle the tahini dressing over the cauliflower, sprinkle it with the sesame seed mixture and serve it while it is still piping hot.

Serves 4

Minted potato salad

600 g (1 lb 5 oz) chat potatoes,
  large ones halved
125 g (½ cup) thick plain yoghurt
1 Lebanese (short) cucumber, grated
  and squeezed dry
15 g (¼ cup) finely chopped mint
  leaves
2 garlic cloves, crushed

Boil or steam the chat potatoes for
10 minutes, or until they are tender,
then leave them to cool. Mix together
the yoghurt, cucumber, mint and
garlic and toss it through the cooled
potatoes. Season well and serve.

Serves 4

Barbecue sauce

2 teaspoons oil
1 small onion, finely chopped
1 tablespoon malt vinegar
1 tablespoon soft brown sugar
80 ml (⅓ cup) tomato sauce
1 tablespoon Worcestershire sauce

Heat the oil in a small pan and cook the onion over low heat for 3 minutes, or until soft, stirring occasionally.

Add the remaining ingredients and bring to the boil. Reduce the heat and simmer for 3 minutes, stirring occasionally. Serve warm or at room temperature. Can be kept, covered and refrigerated, for up to a week.

Serves 4

Dill coleslaw

90 g (⅓ cup) sour cream
2 teaspoons prepared horseradish
1 tablespoon lemon juice
1 tablespoon Dijon mustard
2 tablespoons finely chopped dill
300 g (4 cups) shredded red cabbage
2 carrots, peeled and grated

Put the sour cream, horseradish, lemon juice, mustard and dill in a large bowl and stir it together. Add the cabbage and carrot, toss them together well so that the coleslaw is lightly coated with dressing, and season to taste. Cover and refrigerate until ready to serve.

Serves 6–8

Warm marinated mushroom salad

750 g (1 lb 10 oz) mixed mushrooms
(such as baby button, oyster,
Swiss brown, shiitake and enoki)
2 garlic cloves, finely chopped
½ teaspoon green peppercorns,
crushed
80 ml (⅓ cup) olive oil
80 ml (⅓ cup) orange juice
250 g (9 oz) salad leaves, watercress
or baby spinach leaves
1 teaspoon finely grated orange zest

Trim the mushroom stems and wipe the mushrooms with a damp paper towel. Cut any large mushrooms in half. Mix together the garlic, peppercorns, olive oil and orange juice. Pour over the mushrooms and marinate for about 20 minutes.

Arrange the salad leaves in a large serving dich.

Drain the mushrooms, reserving the marinade. Cook the flat and button mushrooms on a hot, lightly oiled barbecue grill or flat plate for about 2 minutes. Add the softer mushrooms and cook for 1 minute, or until they just soften.

Scatter the mushrooms over the salad leaves and drizzle with the marinade. Sprinkle with orange zest and season well with salt and pepper.

Serves 4

Guacamole

2 ripe avocados, mashed
2½ tablespoons lime juice
3 spring onions (scallions), finely
  sliced
15 g (¼ cup) chopped coriander
  (cilantro) leaves
1 teaspoon finely chopped red chilli

Combine the avocado, lime juice,
spring onion, coriander and chilli, and
season the mixture to taste. Cover the
guacamole with plastic wrap, resting
the plastic directly on the surface of
the mixture, and refrigerate until you
are ready to use it.

Serves 4–6

Chickpea salad

2 large tins chickpeas (see Note)
3 tomatoes
1 red onion, thinly sliced
1 small red capsicum (pepper),
  cut into thin strips
4 spring onions (scallions), cut
  into thin strips
60 g (1 cup) chopped flat-leaf
  (Italian) parsley
2–3 tablespoons chopped mint
  leaves

Dressing
2 tablespoons tahini
2 tablespoons lemon juice
3 tablespoons olive oil
2 garlic cloves, crushed
½ teaspoon ground cumin

Drain the chickpeas and rinse well.
Cut the tomatoes in half and remove
the seeds with a spoon. Dice the
flesh. Mix the red onion, tomato,
capsicum and spring onion in a bowl.
Add the chickpeas, parsley and mint.

To make the dressing, put all the
ingredients in a screw-top jar with
2 tablespoons water, season well and
shake vigorously to make a creamy
liquid. Pour over the salad and toss.

Serves 8

Note: If you prefer, you can use dried
chickpeas, but they will need to be
soaked and cooked first. Use 380 g
(1¾ cups) dried chickpeas and put
in a pan with 3.5 litres water and
3 tablespoons olive oil. Partially cover
and boil for 2½ hours, or until tender.
Rinse, drain well and allow to cool a
little before making the salad.

Baby spinach salad

2 tablespoons olive oil
1 tablespoon lemon juice
150 g (5½ oz) baby spinach leaves
100 g (3½ oz) small black olives
sea salt

Whisk together the olive oil and the lemon juice.

Toss the spinach in a large serving bowl with the olives and the combined olive oil and lemon juice. Season the salad with sea salt and freshly ground black pepper.

Serves 4

Parsley carrots

600 g (1 lb 5 oz) baby carrots
2 teaspoons olive oil
30 g (1 oz) butter
2 tablespoons finely chopped
  flat-leaf (Italian) parsley

Bring a saucepan of salted water to the boil, and blanch the carrots for 3 minutes or until they start to soften. Drain and refresh them under cold water and pat them dry with paper towels. Toss the carrots in olive oil and season with salt and pepper.

When you are nearly ready to serve the main meal, preheat a barbecue chargrill plate to medium heat and cook the carrots for 5 minutes, or until they are charred and golden all over. Toss the carrots with the butter and parsley until they are well coated, season to taste with salt and freshly ground black pepper and serve.

Serves 6–8

Tomato salsa

4 ripe tomatoes, finely diced
40 g (¼ cup) finely chopped red
  onion
25 g (½ cup) chopped coriander
  (cilantro) leaves
1 tablespoon lime juice

Combine the tomato, onion, coriander and lime juice, season to taste, then cover the salsa with plastic wrap and refrigerate. Remove the salsa from the refrigerator 15 minutes before you are ready to use it so the ingredients have time to return to room temperature and their full flavour.

Serves 4

Asian salad

2 sheets nori, cut into 3 cm x 5 mm
(1 1/4 x 1/4 inch) pieces
2 tablespoons seasoned rice wine
vinegar
2 teaspoons lemon juice
1/4 teaspoon sesame oil
2 teaspoons canola oil
60 g (2 1/4 oz) mizuna leaves
60 g (2 1/4 oz) snowpea (mangetout)
shoots
2 Lebanese (short) cucumbers,
shaved
1/2 daikon, shaved

Toast the nori on a preheated
barbecue plate for 5 minutes to
make it crispy.

To make the dressing, whisk together
the vinegar, lemon juice, sesame oil
and canola oil. Toss the mizuna,
snowpea shoots, cucumber, daikon
and nori with the dressing, and serve.

Serves 4

Chargrilled asparagus

500 g (1 lb 2 oz) asparagus
2 garlic cloves, crushed
2 tablespoons balsamic vinegar
2 tablespoons olive oil
50 g (1¾ oz) Parmesan cheese
shavings

Break off the woody ends from the asparagus by gently bending the stems until the tough end snaps away. Cook the asparagus on a hot, lightly oiled barbecue grill or flat plate for 3 minutes, or until bright green and just tender.

To make the dressing, whisk the garlic, vinegar and olive oil. Pour the dressing over the warm asparagus and top with the Parmesan shavings and lots of black pepper.

Serves 4

Barbecued baby potatoes

750 g (1 lb 10 oz) baby potatoes,
  unpeeled
2 tablespoons olive oil
2 tablespoons thyme leaves
2 teaspoons crushed sea salt

Cut any large potatoes in half so that they are all the same size for even cooking. Boil, steam or microwave the potatoes until just tender. Drain and lightly dry with paper towels.

Put the potatoes in a large bowl and add the oil and thyme. Toss gently and leave for 1 hour.

Lightly oil a barbecue flat plate and preheat it to high direct heat. Cook the potatoes for 15 minutes, turning frequently and brushing with the remaining oil and thyme mixture, until golden brown. Sprinkle with salt to serve.

Serves 6

Note: The potatoes can be left in the marinade for up to 2 hours before barbecuing, but should be served as soon as they are cooked.

Cucumber salad

1 telegraph (long) cucumber
1 tablespoon sugar
60 ml (¼ cup) lime juice
1 tablespoon fish sauce
1 red Asian shallot, finely sliced
10 g (⅓ cup) coriander (cilantro)
  leaves
1 small red chilli, seeds removed
  and finely chopped
75 g (2½ oz) snowpea (mangetout)
  shoots

Peel the cucumber, cut it in half lengthways, remove the seeds and cut it into 5 mm (¼ inch) slices. Put the sugar and lime juice in a large bowl, and stir them together until the sugar has dissolved, then add the fish sauce.

Toss the cucumber, shallot, coriander and chilli through the dressing, then cover and refrigerate for 15 minutes. Just before serving, cut the snowpea shoots in half and stir them through the salad.

Serves 4

Ratatouille

1 bulb of garlic
80 ml (⅓ cup) olive oil
6 Roma (plum) tomatoes, halved
lengthways
4 baby eggplants (aubergines), cut
into 1 cm (½ inch) pieces on the
diagonal
3 zucchini (courgettes), cut into 1 cm
(½ inch) pieces on the diagonal
2 red capsicums (peppers), seeded
and cut into wedges
2 red onions, cut into 1 cm (½ inch)
thick rounds
2 tablespoons balsamic vinegar

Trim the top of the garlic bulb so that
the cloves are just exposed, drizzle
1 teaspoon of olive oil over the cut
end and wrap the bulb in foil. Put the
garlic in a barbecue that has been
preheated to medium indirect heat
and cook for 30 minutes, or until it
has softened.

Lightly brush the vegetables with
2 tablespoons of olive oil and add
them to the barbecue when the
garlic has been cooking for about
15 minutes. Cook the vegetables for
5–8 minutes on each side, or until
they are marked and cooked through,
then put them in a large bowl.

Squeeze the garlic cloves out of their
skins and add to the vegetables. Mix
the balsamic vinegar and remaining
olive oil together, gently toss it with
the ratatouille and season well.

Serves 6

Damper

375 g (3 cups) self-raising flour
1–2 teaspoons salt
90 g (3¼ oz) butter, melted
125 ml (½ cup) milk
milk, extra, to glaze
flour, extra, to dust

Preheat the oven to 210°C (415°F/ Gas 6–7). Grease a baking tray. Sift the flour and salt into a bowl and make a well. Combine the butter, milk and 125 ml (½ cup) water and pour into the well. Stir with a knife until just combined. Turn the dough onto a lightly floured surface and knead for 20 seconds, or until smooth. Place the dough on the baking tray and press out to a 15 cm (6 inch) circle.

Using a sharp pointed knife, score the dough into 6 sections about 1 cm (½ inch) deep. Brush with milk, then dust with flour. Bake for 10 minutes.

Reduce the oven temperature to 180°C (350°F/Gas 4) and bake the damper for another 15 minutes, or until the damper is golden and sounds hollow when the surface is tapped. Serve with butter.

Makes 1 damper

Note: Damper is the Australian version of soda bread, and is traditionally served warm with slatherings of golden syrup (dark corn syrup). If you prefer, you can make four rounds instead of one large damper and slightly reduce the cooking time. Cut two slashes in the form of a cross on the top.

Corn bread

125 g (1 cup) self-raising flour
150 g (1 cup) fine cornmeal
1 teaspoon salt
1 egg
250 ml (1 cup) buttermilk
60 ml (¼ cup) oil

Preheat the oven to 220°C (425°F/ Gas 7). Generously grease a 20 cm (8 inch) cast iron frying pan with an ovenproof or screw off handle, or round cake tin, with oil. Place in the oven to heat while making the batter.

Sift the flour into a bowl, add the cornmeal and salt and make a well in the centre. Whisk together the egg, buttermilk and oil, add to the dry ingredients and stir until just combined. Take care not to overbeat.

Spoon into the hot cast iron pan or cake tin and bake for 25 minutes, or until firm to the touch and golden brown. Cut into wedges and serve.

Makes 1 loaf

Rosettas

2 teaspoons dried yeast
1 teaspoon sugar
560 g (4½ cups) unbleached plain
   (all-purpose) flour, sifted
1 teaspoon salt
50 g (1¾ oz) butter, softened
60 ml (¼ cup) olive oil
1½ tablespoons caster (superfine)
   sugar
milk, to glaze
plain (all-purpose) flour, extra,
   to dust

Grease two baking trays. Place the yeast, sugar and 125 ml (½ cup) warm water in a small bowl and stir well. Leave in a warm, draught-free place for 10 minutes, or until bubbles appear on the surface. The mixture should be frothy and slightly increased in volume. If your yeast doesn't foam it is dead, so you will have to discard it and start again.

Set aside 30 g (¼ cup) of the flour and put the rest in a large bowl with the salt. Make a well in the centre. Add the yeast mixture, butter, oil, sugar and 315 ml (1¼ cups) warm water. Stir with a wooden spoon, until the dough leaves the side of the bowl and forms a rough, sticky ball. Turn out onto a floured surface. Knead for 10 minutes, or until the dough is smooth and elastic. Add enough of the reserved flour, if necessary, to make a smooth dough. Place in a large, lightly oiled bowl and brush the surface with melted butter or oil. Cover with plastic wrap and leave in a warm place for 1 hour, or until well risen.

Punch down the dough, then knead for 1 minute. Divide into 10 portions and shape each into a smooth ball. Place the balls 5 cm (2 inches) apart on the trays. Using a 3 cm (1¼ inch) round cutter, press a 1 cm (½ inch) deep indent into the centre of each ball. With a sharp knife, score five evenly spaced, 1 cm (½ inch) deep cuts down the side of each roll. Cover with plastic wrap or a damp tea towel and leave in a warm place for 1 hour, or until well risen.

Preheat the oven to 180°C (350°F/ Gas 4). Brush the rolls with milk and sift a fine layer of the extra flour over them. Bake for 25 minutes, or until golden. Rotate the trays in the oven if one tray is browning faster than the other. Cool on a rack.

Makes 10 rolls

Note: These are best eaten on the day of cooking but can be frozen for up to 1 month.

Beer bread

435 g (3½ cups) self-raising flour
1 teaspoon salt
1 teaspoon caster (superfine) sugar
1 teaspoon dill seeds
40 g (1½ oz) butter, melted
375 ml (1½ cups) beer
plain (all-purpose) flour, for kneading
dill seeds, extra
coarse sea salt

Preheat the oven to 190°C (375°F/ Gas 5). Lightly grease a baking tray. Sift the flour and salt into a large bowl. Add the sugar and dill seeds and combine. Make a well in the centre and add the butter and beer all at once. Using a wooden spoon, quickly mix to form a soft dough.

Turn out onto a floured surface, sprinkling extra flour on your hands and on the surface of the dough. Knead for 30–45 seconds. Elongate the ball slightly, flatten a little, and with the blunt end of a large knife press down 2 cm (¾ inch) along the centre. Brush the surface with water, and sprinkle liberally with the extra dill seeds and sea salt.

Bake for 20 minutes, then reduce the oven to 180°C (350°F/Gas 4) and bake for another 30 minutes, or until the bread sounds hollow when tapped. Remove from the oven, place on a wire rack and leave to cool.

Makes 1 loaf

Note: This bread is best eaten on the day of baking and it freezes well for up to a week.

Desserts

Camembert with port-soaked raisins

2 tablespoons raisins
2 tablespoons port
365 g (12 oz) whole Camembert
   cheese
canola oil spray
almond bread, to serve

Put the raisins and port in a small saucepan over high heat until they just come to the boil, then allow the mixture to cool for about 30 minutes.

Cut a circular lid from the top of the Camembert, leaving a 2 cm (3/4 inch) border. Carefully remove the lid, and scoop out the soft cheese with a teaspoon, leaving the base intact. Put the raisins in the hole and top with the cheese, squashing it down so that as much as possible fits back into the cavity, then replace the lid.

Lightly spray a double layer of foil with canola spray and wrap the Camembert to form a sealed parcel. Preheat a barbecue flat plate to low direct heat and cook the parcel for 8–10 minutes, or until it is heated through and soft. Make sure the heat stays low, or the rind will go brown and burn. Serve with the almond bread.

Serves 4

Note: After cooking your main feast, there should be just enough heat left in the barbecue to warm the Camembert for this delicious dessert.

Berry and marshmallow gratin

600 g (1 lb 5 oz) mixed seasonal
  berries (strawberries, raspberries,
  blueberries, blackberries) (see Note)
2 tablespoons raspberry liqueur
150 g (5½ oz) pink and white
  marshmallows
vanilla ice cream

Put the berries and raspberry liqueur in a bowl, stir them gently to coat the berries and transfer them to a 1.5 litre ceramic ovenproof dish. Top the berries with the marshmallows, making sure they are evenly distributed over the surface.

Preheat a covered or kettle barbecue to medium–high indirect heat and put the dish in the middle of the barbecue. Cook for 8–10 minutes or until the berries are bubbling and the marshmallow has puffed up and is starting to melt. Serve the gratin immediately with a big scoop of ice cream, but take care to not burn your mouth on the berries, which will be very hot.

Serves 6

Note: If it is not berry season, and your berries are not as sweet as they should be, add a little caster (superfine) sugar with the liqueur. Use strawberries in a smaller proportion to the other berries as they tend to release a lot of liquid.

Grilled panettone with peaches

125 g (½ cup) caster (superfine) sugar
½ vanilla bean, halved and scraped
1 tablespoon Grand Marnier
4 ripe peaches
oil, for brushing
4 large slices panettone
80 g (⅓ cup) crème fraîche

Put the sugar, vanilla bean and 60 ml (¼ cup) water in a small saucepan and stir over low heat until the sugar has dissolved. Simmer the mixture, without stirring it, for 10 minutes, then remove it from the heat, stir in the Grand Marnier and keep it warm.

Dip the peaches into a saucepan of boiling water for 5 seconds then refresh them under cold water and remove the skins, which should slip off easily. Cut the peaches in half, remove the stone and lightly brush the cut side with oil. Preheat a barbecue chargrill plate to medium direct heat and grill the peaches, cut-side down, for 5 minutes, or until golden and warmed through. Grill the panettone for 30 seconds to 1 minute on each side, or until it is marked and lightly toasted. The panettone will brown very quickly, so be careful to not burn it. Arrange the grilled peaches over the panettone, drizzle with the vanilla syrup and serve with a scoop of crème fraîche.

Serves 4

Pear and hazelnut crêpes with cinnamon sugar

Crêpes
250 g (2 cups) plain (all-purpose)
   flour
3 eggs
375 ml (1½ cups) milk
60 g (2¼ oz) butter, melted
melted butter, extra, for cooking

Filling
500 g (2 cups) cream cheese
2 tablespoons icing (confectioners')
   sugar, sifted
80 g (⅔ cup) hazelnuts, toasted,
   skinned and roughly chopped
150 g (⅔ cup) candied peel
2 teaspoons finely grated lemon
   zest
2 tablespoons Frangelico or Poire
   William
1 large firm green pear, cored and
   cut into 1 cm (½ inch) dice

2 tablespoons caster (superfine)
   sugar
1 teaspoon ground cinnamon

To make the crêpe batter, sift the flour into a bowl with a pinch of salt and make a well. Gradually whisk in the combined eggs and milk until the batter is smooth, then stir in the melted butter. Strain the batter into a jug, cover and refrigerate it for 1 hour. The consistency should be similar to thin cream, so add a little more milk if it looks too thick.

To make the filling, beat the cream cheese and icing sugar in a bowl until smooth. Add the hazelnuts, peel, zest and liqueur, and stir it all together. Gently stir in the diced pear and refrigerate the filling until you are ready to use it.

Heat an 18 cm (7 inch) crêpe or non-stick frying pan over low–medium heat and brush it with butter. Pour 60 ml (¼ cup) of batter into the pan, and swirl it around so that the bottom of the pan is thinly covered. Cook the crêpe for 1 minute or until the edges just begin to curl, then turn it over and cook the other side for 30 seconds. Slide the crêpe out of the pan onto a plate and continue with the remaining batter, stacking the crêpes as you go.

Put 2 heaped tablespoons of the filling in the middle of each crêpe, fold two opposite sides in to the middle and flatten the mixture slightly,

then fold in the other two sides to enclose the filling.

Preheat a barbecue flat plate to low direct heat and cook the crêpe parcels for 3–4 minutes on each side, or until they are golden and crisp, and the filling is warmed through. Transfer the parcels to serving plates, sprinkle with the combined caster sugar and cinnamon, and serve immediately.

Makes 12 crêpes

Note: If you are making the crêpes in advance, stack them between sheets of greaseproof paper to stop them from sticking to each other. Do not refrigerate.

Amaretti-stuffed apples with vanilla ricotta

2 tablespoons sultanas
2 tablespoons amaretto
10 small amaretti biscuits (about
   60 g/2¼ oz), crushed
2 tablespoons slivered almonds,
   toasted
1 tablespoon sugar
2½ tablespoons butter, melted
4 Granny Smith apples

Vanilla ricotta
½ vanilla bean
2 tablespoons icing (confectioners')
   sugar
250 g (1 cup) ricotta cheese

Soak the sultanas in the amaretto for 15 minutes or until they are softened, then add them to the crushed amaretti with the amaretto, slivered almonds, sugar and 2 tablespoons of melted butter.

Scrape the seeds out of the vanilla bean and add them and the icing sugar to the ricotta. Use an electric beater to beat the mixture until the ricotta is smooth and creamy.

Remove the apple cores and enough fruit from around the core to make a hole about 2.5 cm (1 inch) across. Stuff the hole with the amaretto mixture, brush the apples with the remaining melted butter and wrap them securely in foil. Preheat a kettle or covered barbecue to low–medium indirect heat, put the apples on the barbecue and cook them, covered, for 15–20 minutes, or until they are tender. Serve with a big scoop of the vanilla ricotta.

Serves 4

Note: Vanilla ricotta is a delicious alternative to whipped or double cream to serve with desserts.

Pineapple with brown sugar glaze and toasted coconut

1 pineapple
95 g (½ cup) dark brown sugar
½ teaspoon vanilla essence
1 tablespoon Galliano
60 g (2¼ oz) butter
2 tablespoons coconut flakes,
 toasted
vanilla ice cream

Peel the pineapple and remove all the eyes, then slice it lengthways into quarters and remove the core. Cut into long 1 cm (½ inch) wide wedges.

Put the brown sugar, vanilla essence and 2 teaspoons water in a small saucepan and cook it over low–medium heat for 5 minutes, or until the sugar has dissolved. Remove the pan from the heat, add the Galliano, then return the pan to the heat and simmer the mixture for 3 minutes. Whisk in the butter and continue to simmer the mixture over low heat for 15 minutes, or until smooth and thick.

Preheat a barbecue chargrill plate to medium direct heat, brush the pineapple with the brown sugar glaze, and grill for 2–3 minutes, or until grill marks appear. Arrange the pineapple pieces on a serving platter, top with the glaze and the toasted coconut, and serve with vanilla ice cream.

Serves 6

Coconut pancakes with grilled bananas and syrup

150 g (5½ oz) palm sugar, roughly
  chopped, or soft brown sugar
2 tablespoons lime juice
125 g (1 cup) plain (all-purpose)
  flour
45 g (¼ cup) rice flour
125 g (½ cup) caster (superfine)
  sugar
45 g (½ cup) desiccated coconut
500 ml (2 cups) coconut milk
2 eggs, lightly beaten
4 bananas, sliced thickly on the
  diagonal
2 tablespoons dark brown sugar
50 g (1¾ oz) butter, plus extra,
  for cooking
30 g (½ cup) shredded coconut,
  toasted
1 lime, cut into wedges

Put the palm sugar in a small, heavy-based saucepan with 125 ml (½ cup) water and stir it over low heat for 5 minutes, or until the sugar has dissolved. Increase the heat to medium and let it simmer, without stirring, for 15 minutes, or until the liquid becomes a thick, sticky syrup. Stir in the lime juice and keep the syrup warm.

Sift the plain and rice flour together, add the caster sugar and desiccated coconut, and stir it all together. Make a well in the middle and pour in the combined coconut milk and egg, beating until the mixture is smooth.

Preheat a barbecue flat plate to low–medium direct heat. Toss the bananas in the dark brown sugar and grill them around the cooler edges of the flat plate, dotting each piece with butter. Cook the banana, turning the pieces occasionally, for 4–5 minutes, or until it begins to soften and brown. Melt a little of the extra butter in the middle of the plate and pour on 60 ml (¼ cup) of the pancake mixture, using the back of a spoon to spread it out to a 15 cm (6 inch) circle. Cook the pancake for 2–3 minutes, or until the underside is golden, then turn it over and cook the other side for another minute. As each pancake is cooked, transfer it to a plate and cover it with a tea towel to keep it warm. Add more butter to the hot plate as necessary and keep going until all of the pancake mixture has been used.

Fold each pancake into quarters and put two on each serving plate. Top with grilled banana, drizzle with a little palm sugar syrup and sprinkle with the coconut. Serve with lime wedges.

Serves 4

Fruit skewers with rum butter

1 peach, peeled, stoned and cut
  into 8 pieces
1 mango, peeled, stoned and cut
  into 8 pieces
8 strawberries, hulled and halved
160 g (5½ oz) papaya, cut into
  8 pieces
160 g (5½ oz) pineapple, cut into
  8 pieces
2 bananas, cut into 2 cm (¾ inch)
  pieces
185 ml (¾ cup) dark rum
60 g (⅓ cup) dark brown sugar
1 tablespoon butter
ice cream, to serve

Put the peach, mango, strawberries, papaya, pineapple and banana in a bowl with the rum and sugar, and stir gently until all of the fruit is coated in the marinade. Cover and refrigerate the bowl for 1 hour.

Soak eight wooden skewers in cold water for 1 hour. Drain the marinade into a small, heavy-based saucepan and thread the fruit onto the skewers. Make sure each skewer has a good mix of fruits and that the pieces are not crowded, otherwise they won't cook evenly.

Bring the marinade to the boil over medium heat, then reduce the heat and simmer for 5 minutes, or until it is reduced and syrupy. Remove the pan from the heat and whisk in the butter until it becomes smooth and glossy.

Preheat a flat barbecue grill plate to medium direct heat and cook the skewers for 5–8 minutes on each side, or until they are golden, basting them all over with the rum glaze during the last minute of cooking. Arrange the skewers on a serving plate, drizzle them with the rum glaze and serve warm with ice cream.

Serves 4

Basics

Types of barbecue

There are two main methods of cooking on a barbecue. The first is to cook food over direct heat, such as over a wood fire or barbecue fuel briquettes located directly under a grill or plate. The food must be turned during cooking so that it cooks evenly on both sides.

The other method is to use indirect heat, for which you need a barbecue with some kind of hood or cover. This method of cooking works a bit like an oven, by circulating the heat around the food, and it is mainly used for roasting larger cuts of meat, giving them a distinctive barbecue flavour.

Wood-burning fixed barbecues are the traditional,

backyard barbecue — usually a fairly simple construction in the form of an elevated grill plate with a fire burning underneath. Although easy to use and available to anyone with clear space, a few bricks and a grill, the basic design lends itself only to fairly simple methods of cooking. Heat regulation is usually achieved by adjusting the fire and waiting for it to reach the right temperature, although it's preferable to let the flames die down and cook over a pile of glowing embers which give off a more constant heat.

Kettle barbecues are portable,

come in a range of sizes and are designed for both direct and indirect cooking. A kettle barbecue has a rounded base which holds barbecue fuel briquettes on a metal grill. If you want to cook with direct heat, simply grill the food over the coals. If you want to cook using the indirect method, arrange the briquettes in two piles on opposite sides of the bottom grill and put a drip-tray between them before inserting the top grill. To give the heat a boost, open the vents in the outer shell of the barbecue — this will allow air to circulate, making the briquettes burn faster and hotter. To keep the temperature a little cooler, leave the vents closed.

Gas barbecues are available in

a huge variety of sizes and shapes, from small portables to huge, wagon-style barbecues that come with a hood, rotisserie and workbench on the side. They are convenient and simple to operate, usually requiring only 10 minutes or so to heat up, and the turn of a knob to regulate temperature. Some work by means of a flame under the barbecue plate, while others use the flame to heat a bed of reusable volcanic rock. If your barbecue has a lid or hood, you can also cook using indirect heat.

Electric barbecues operate

on a principle similar to that of gas barbecues, by heating the grill plate on which the food is cooked. They can be less convenient than a gas barbecue as they require access to an electricity outlet and the heat produced may not be as even or as strong as that produced by a gas or solid-fuel barbecue.

Methods of cooking

Indirect and direct are the main cooking methods when you are using a barbecue. Make sure you set up your barbecue properly to shorten cooking times and make sure that all your lovingly prepared meals are perfectly cooked.

For direct cooking

kettle barbecue, start the barbecue and let the briquettes burn for about 45 minutes before you begin cooking. For a medium–hot barbecue, use about 60, for a lower temperature, about 45 briquettes should be enough. If you need to lower the temperature when the fire is already set, just spritz the coals with a light spray of water, but if you want to increase the heat, you will need to add more briquettes and wait for the heat to develop.

gas or electric barbecue, light the barbecue and let it heat for about 10 minutes before cooking.

For indirect cooking

kettle barbecue, start the barbecue (putting the fuel on each side to leave room for the drip tray) and leave the fire to develop for about 45 minutes. Put a drip tray between the coals and sit the top grill in place. Position the food so that it is over the drip tray and cover it with the lid. Keep the bottom vents open so that the heat circulates evenly, and don't open the lid unless it's really necessary — the more often the heat is allowed to escape, the longer your cooking time will be.

gas or electric barbecue, it's best to check the manufacturers' instructions on how to set up your barbecue for indirect cooking. In general, the outside burners are set to medium–low and the food sits in the middle of the barbecue. This means that the heat can circulate around the meat without burning it underneath.

BBQ tips

● Food cooked on a grill plate can also be cooked on an open grill provided it is large enough not to fall through the holes.

● Food cooked on an open grill may also be cooked on a grill plate.

● Invest in a small fire extinguisher, in case of emergency.

● For best results, bring the meat to room temperature before cooking it, but it is not advisable to leave it sitting at room temperature for more than 20 minutes.

● Always make sure that your barbecue is clean before lighting it. If possible, clean it out as soon as it is cool enough, brushing or scraping the grill plates and discarding ash and embers.

● Assemble all the equipment you will need before you start cooking so that you won't have to leave the food unattended.

● Make sure that the barbecue is in a sheltered position and on a level surface, away from wooden fences, overhanging trees or anything else that may be flammable.

● Brush or spray the barbecue with oil before lighting it in case the oil comes in contact with the flame and flares up. To stop food from sticking, brush it with oil just before cooking it, make sure the grill plate is the correct temperature and don't turn the food until the surface of the food has cooked and 'released' itself naturally from the grill.

● If you wish to use the marinade to baste, you must boil it, then let it simmer for at least 5 minutes before basting so that any bacteria from the raw meat are not transferred to the cooked meat.

● If you are basting the food with a sugary glaze, apply it only in the last 10 minutes of cooking, as it will tend to burn on the grill.

● Always soak wooden skewers for an hour before use to prevent them from charring on the grill.

● Salt meat just before barbecuing as salt will quickly draw moisture out of the meat if it is left.

Cooking time guide

The cooking temperature in a kettle or covered barbecue is not always constant, so we've provided these times to use as a guide (500 g = 1 lb 2 oz).

Beef per 500 g	with a bone	boneless
rare	15 minutes	10 minutes
medium	20 minutes	15 minutes
well done	25 minutes	20 minutes

Leg of lamb per 500 g

medium rare	10–15 minutes
medium	20–25 minutes
well done	30 minutes

Pork
allow 30 minutes per 500 g
Pork should be cooked through, but not overcooked or the flesh will be dry. Test that it is ready by inserting a skewer into the thickest part of the pork, or close to the bone; the juices should be clear with no trace of pink.

Poultry
allow 20–25 minutes per 500 g
It's important that chicken is cooked right through with no pink flesh or juices inside. Check by inserting a skewer between the thigh and the body through to the bone; the juices should run clear.

Fish
allow 20–25 minutes per 500 g
Different varieties of fish require different cooking times. Tuna and salmon steaks are often cooked medium rare, as the flesh can become dry if cooked through. Depending on thickness, they may only need a few minutes on each side over direct heat. Most other fish are served cooked through. It is important to remove them from the barbecue as soon as they are ready, as residual heat in the flesh will continue to cook the meat. Test by inserting a thin-bladed knife into the thickest part of the fish; it will be ready when the flesh flakes cleanly.

Glossary

baste to spoon or brush cooking juices or other fat over food during cooking to prevent it from drying out, or to help with heat transfer.

brown to pan-fry, bake, grill or roast food (often meat) so the outer surface turns a golden brown colour.

caramelize to cook until sugars, which either exist naturally in the food or are added (for example in a marinade), become golden brown.

chargrill a heavy metal plate with slotted grill bars which allows the food to be directly exposed to the heat and fire below for a true barbecue flavour. It also refers to this method of cooking.

charred food cooked on a chargrill until the surface is blackened.

core to remove the core from fruit by using a corer or a small knife.

covered barbecue refers to a barbecue that has a fitted lid which may be closed to make it suitable for roasting or slow cooking.

dice to chop food into very small, even cubes. Use a very sharp knife to do this.

drip tray used in kettle barbecues for indirect cooking. It is placed between the fuel briquettes to catch any dripping juices.

dry-fry to cook spices in a dry frying pan until they become fragrant. Keep a close eye on spices cooked in this way, as they can burn in a very short space of time.

fillet to cut the meat, fish or poultry away from the bone. Also refers to the cut of meat, commonly taken from the top half of an animal's leg.

flat grill plate a heavy, flat metal plate set over a heat source which doesn't allow the flames from the barbecue to actually touch the food. This means that there are no flare-ups caused by dripping juices or fat.

glaze to coat food with a liquid as it is cooking. A glaze adds flavour, colour and shine.

grease to lightly coat a tin or dish with oil or melted butter to prevent food from sticking.

heavy-based saucepan usually has a copper lining in the base which allows for even and constant distribution of heat across the whole base of the pan.

kettle barbecue refers to a rounded barbecue with a lid.

marinate to tenderize and flavour food (usually meat) by leaving it in an acidulated seasoned liquid (marinade).

non-metallic dish a ceramic or glass dish which will not react with any acids in the foods stored or marinated in it.

parboil to partially cook a food in boiling water before some other form of cooking. Most commonly used for roast potatoes, which are parboiled before going in to the roasting tin.

purée food blended or processed to a pulp.

reduce to boil or simmer liquid in an uncovered pan so that some of the liquid evaporates, causing the mixture to become thicker and more concentrated in flavour.

rest to allow meat to sit, covered, for a period of time after it has cooked before slicing it. This enables the muscle fibres to relax and so retain the juices when cut.

rub a mixture of dried herbs and spices used as a dry marinade for foods, usually meat.

score to make incisions with a knife (usually into fish or meat) in a crossed pattern, without cutting all the way through. This ensures even cooking through thicker sections of the food.

shred to cut food into small, narrow strips, either by hand, or using a grater or food processor with a shredding disc. Cooked meat may be shredded by pulling it apart with forks or your fingers.

simmer to cook liquid, or food in a liquid, over low heat, just below boiling point. The surface of the liquid should be moving, with a few small bubbles coming to the surface.

skim to remove fat or scum that comes to the surface of a liquid.

smoke adding fragrant woodchips to the barbecue heat source to produce smoke which will impart a distinctive flavour to the food as it cooks. Works best with barbecue briquettes.

strain to remove solids from a liquid by pouring it through a sieve. The solids are discarded, unless otherwise specified.

Index

Index

Index

Recipe Writers: Vanessa Broadfoot, Ross Dobson, Kathleen Gandy, Jane Lawson, Christine Osmond, Rebecca Truda.

Special thanks to MUD Australia, Major & Tom and Kif Kaf Designs, who supplied props and accessories for photography, and Woodland Home Products Pty Ltd and Weber Australia for providing the barbecues.

Published by Murdoch Books Pty Limited

Designer: Michelle Cutler (internals); Marylouise Brammer (cover)
Photographers: Jared Fowler (chapter openers); Stuart Scott (cover)
Stylists: Cherise Koch; (chapter openers); Louise Bickle (cover)
Editor: Gordana Trifunovic Production: Elizabeth Malcolm

Chief Executive: Juliet Rogers
Publishing Director: Kay Scarlett
Commissioning Editor: Lynn Lewis
Senior Designer: Heather Menzies

National Library of Australia Cataloguing-in-Publication Data
Title: BBQ food/editor, Lynn Lewis. ISBN 9781741965315 (pbk.)
Series: New chunky. Includes index. Subjects: Barbecue cookery. 641.5784

Printed by 1010 Printing International Ltd
PRINTED IN CHINA
First printed 2003. This edition 2009.

For fan-forced ovens, set the oven temperature to 20°C (35°F) lower than indicated in the recipe.
We have used 20 ml tablespoon measures. IMPORTANT: Those who might be at risk from the effects
of salmonella poisoning (the elderly, pregnant women, young children and those suffering from immune
deficiency diseases) should consult their GP with any concerns about eating raw eggs.

Cover credits: White flower dinner plates, White Home. Starburst fabric in brown,
Prints Charming. Plain dyed napkin in chocolate, Dandi. Marimekko Kaivo fabric in colour 3
(black, brown and white), Roundabout. Designers Guild Anichov Aqua fabric, No Chintz.
Iittala Mango Cutlery, Design Mode International. Front flap: Japanese floral print fabric, No Chintz.

A catalogue record for this book is available from the British Library.

Published by:
AUSTRALIA
Murdoch Books Pty Ltd
Pier 8/9, 23 Hickson Road,
Millers Point NSW 2000
Phone: + 61 (0) 2 8220 2000
Fax: + 61 (0) 2 8220 2558
www.murdochbooks.com.au

UK
Murdoch Books UK Ltd
Erico House, 6th Floor North,
93-99 Upper Richmond Rd,
Putney, London SW15 2TG
Phone: + 44 (0) 20 8785 5995
Fax: + 44 (0) 20 8785 5985
www.murdochbooks.co.uk